Nathan G. Burgess

The Photograph and ambrotype Manual

A practical Treatise on the Art of taking positive and negative Photographs on

Paper and Glass. Seventh Edition

Nathan G. Burgess

The Photograph and ambrotype Manual
A practical Treatise on the Art of taking positive and negative Photographs on Paper and Glass. Seventh Edition

ISBN/EAN: 9783337142759

Printed in Europe, USA, Canada, Australia, Japan

Cover: Foto ©ninafisch / pixelio.de

More available books at **www.hansebooks.com**

THE PHOTOGRAPH AND AMBROTYPE MANUAL:

A PRACTICAL TREATISE

ON THE ART OF TAKING

POSITIVE AND NEGATIVE PHOTOGRAPHS ON PAPER AND GLASS,

COMMONLY KNOWN AS PHOTOGRAPHY,

IN ALL ITS BRANCHES;

CONTAINING ALL THE VARIOUS RECIPES PRACTISED BY THE MOST SUCCESSFUL OPERATORS IN THE UNITED STATES.

BY N. G. BURGESS,

PRACTICAL PHOTOGRAPHER, AND MANUFACTURER OF CHEMICALS FOR THE ART.

SEVENTH EDITION.

NEW YORK:
HUBBARD, BURGESS & CO.,
78 READE AND 99 CHURCH STREETS.
LONDON: TRÜBNER & CO.
1861.

Entered according to Act of Congress, in the year 1858,

By NATHAN G. BURGESS,

In the Clerk's Office of the District Court of the United States for the Southern District of New York.

PREFACE.

The publication of the Ambrotype Manual, by the author of this work, a short time since, and the great demand for the same, has induced him to enlarge that work by the addition of the practice of Photography in all its branches.

It may not be inappropriate at the present time to refer to the progress of this wonderful art, since its first advent in 1839, and to note its tendencies and its effects, to trace its leading features and results up to its present high position in the scientific world; and, finally, to mark out the commanding results which it is destined yet to achieve in its onward progress to perfection.

The Photographic Art was ushered into the world on the day when the immortal Daguerre, in 1839, announced his sublime discovery to the

French savans, and it has steadily progressed from that day to the present time.

It has made many strides towards perfection, and has astonished all with its accomplishments. In the short space of eighteen years, what has it not done?

From the small and almost imperceptible impression upon the silver plate first exhibited by Daguerre, which could only be seen at a certain angle of light, and that very dimly, and of a blueish cold tone, to the magnificent photograph of the size of life, with all the perfect delineations of light and shade, what a wonderful advance! And these great improvements have been so gradual, that few, if any, could mark the changes. Yet all will acknowledge, that the art is just now beginning to attest its true worth, for we now begin to receive the homage of all true lovers of art. The day has dawned in which the photographer can command even the service of the artist, whose highest pride should be to copy nature in all her works. For now we can exhibit true works of art drawn with the pencilings of the sun's rays, and drawn with such an unerring correctness that it were sacrilege to touch it with the hand of the artist. It defies the artist's skill. It fairly outvies the creations of a Raphael or a Rubens in portraiture, and in the other certain works of the pencil.

The Photographic Art has become of such importance in this country, that many persons have embarked large amounts of capital in the manufacture of materials for the use of the photographic artist. The inducement has been fully warranted from the fact that all these persons who have invested in this branch of commerce have been fully rewarded.

In view of these facts, it is thought proper and necessary to embody in this edition of the work a set of full and complete practical formulæ for the production of all kinds of Photographs on paper, as well as those on glass, known as Ambrotypes. The aim will be to give only such known receipts as have been in actual practice by the author and others, and to explain them in the plainest and most explicit manner possible, in order that the least practised operator may reap the benefit from the perusal of the work, as those of more mature experience.

The practice of the art of taking Photographs on paper has been attended with very diverse results in the United States, owing in a great degree to the fact that most persons who have embarked in it have heretofore been Daguerreian artists. They imagined that it only required the necessary skill and experience of a Daguerreian artist to render them good Photographers. But this has been soon found to be a fallacy. There are many who are skilful in the process known as the Daguerreotype, who can produce specimens of that art which would do credit to the profession, who nevertheless utterly fail in this higher branch of Photography. The reason is obvious. They have vainly imagined that only the same care was necessary in the paper process that was demanded in the manipulation of the silver plate. But how soon have their hopes of success been blasted! Where the ordinary care bestowed upon a Daguerreotype would produce satisfactory results, the same care upon a Photograph on paper would produce a worthless picture. Hence we see the necessity of looking into a higher range of art for the perfection of this branch. And as we approach near the goal of perfection in this sublime art, so much the more does it demand of its votaries greater sacrifices on the altar of patience and perseverance, more nearly resembling the long and weary road of the successful painter, who rises in his profession through many years of patient toil, with his pencil and his pallet, to the highest eminence.

And the day may not be far distant when only those who have been for many long and weary years followers of the Photographic Art, shall become masters of their profession.

It is well, therefore, to fully comprehend the greatness of the task one assumes who embarks in this profession. And to become a perfect master of it, will require all the known resources of his perseverance. Therefore such aids as may be found in the experience of others, will be given here, and it is trusted may be found of essential service to those who may purchase the work and follow the art as a profession.

To the amateurs this work will no doubt be acceptable as a practical treatise, leading them into the more intricate fields of practice not found in scientific works on kindred subjects.

Fortunately for this beautiful art, the number of amateurs is increasing in the United States, and we trust they may continue to augment until the number shall equal those of England and other European countries. For like all beautiful arts, the tempting field of pleasurable labor here opened, is beckoning onwards a host of fellow-laborers, which will render the task of ultimate success of very easy accomplishment; and it is trusted they will emulate those artists in England who have so willingly opened their stores of knowledge to the photographic world, so that all may reap the benefit of their valued experience.

CONTENTS.

	PAGE.
PREFACE	3
INTRODUCTION	9

CHAPTER I.

History and Progress of the Photographic Art—Its Introduction into the United States—The Discovery or Uses of the various Chemicals—Positive Photographs on Glass.................. 19

CHAPTER II.

Theory of the Photographic Process—Negative and Positive Pictures—Negatives on Paper and on Glass—Positives on Glass—Theory of the Positive and the Negative Process............. 30

NEGATIVE PROCESS.

CHAPTER I.

On the Practice of the Negative Process through all its details—The Manipulations—Cleaning the Plate—Coating with Collodion—Drying the same—Time in the Camera—Developing—Re-developing for Intensity—Varnishing the Negative—Frames or Shelves for Negatives—General Remarks on the Manipulation of the Negative Process—Arrangement of the Light—Use of the Camera, &c., &c. 39

CHAPTER II.

The Nitrate of Silver Bath for Negatives—Preparation of the same—Formation of the Iodide of Silver for the Nitrate Bath—On the practice of the Negative Bath—Observations on the use of the Negative Bath—On the Intensity of the Negative—Color of the Negative, &c., &c..................................... 43

CHAPTER III.

On Photographic Printing—Salting Solutions—Salting the Paper—Silvering the Paper with Ammonia Nitrate of Silver—Plain Silver Solution—To prepare the Albumen for Paper Positives—Silvering Albumen Paper—On the practice of printing Negatives—Toning or fixing the Print—Washing the Positive Prints—Drying the Pictures—Varnishing and Mounting the Prints............ 56

CHAPTER IV.

To copy Daguerreotypes and other Pictures into Photographs—On Enlarging Pictures—To enlarge Pictures from Daguerreotypes, Ambrotypes, or Photographs; and to produce Photographs from them—To make Life-size Photographs on Paper—Iron Photographs, or Instantaneous Printing—On taking Stereoscope Pictures, Photographic Views, &c., &c............................ 69

CHAPTER V.

On the Preparation of Negative Collodions—The Formulæ for Negative Collodions—Mixing various Collodions—Dissolving the Iodides—Double Iodide Collodions—The celebrated German Process complete—The Negative Developing Solutions—Re-developing Process—Bichloride of Mercury as a Re-developer—Fixing Solution—The Toning Baths—The Ammonia Nitrate of Silver Solution... 81

CHAPTER VI.

Details of the various Recipes in the Photographic Process—Quick Method of Silvering and Printing Paper—Best Method of Salting Paper—Test for good Collodion or Gun-Cotton—Varnish for Positives on Paper—Instantaneous Printing Process—New Method of

CONTENTS. 11

varnishing Positives—To restore Prints that have changed color—Cleaning Glass Plates—To varnish Negatives—Dextrine Paste for mounting Photographs—Gum-Arabic and Gelatine—To restore Silver from Old Solutions—To remove Water from Collodion, and to purify it—Test of Hyposulphite of Silver in Positive Prints—Printing various Backgrounds.............................. 97

CHAPTER VII.

Hints and Suggestions in regard to the Negative Process—Imperfections peculiar to Negatives—How to avoid them—Cautions in taking Negatives—Hints and Suggestions in regard to printing Positives on Paper—Cautions in regard to them—Imperfections found in Positives—How to avoid them..................... 111

AMBROTYPE PROCESS.

CHAPTER VIII.

The Camera—Plate-holders necessary for the Camera—Preparing the Glasses—Plate-blocks for holding the Glasses—Cleaning Substances—Cleaning the Glasses—Cleaning old Glasses—Removing the Varnish—Holding Glasses after they are cleaned—Glasses used a number of times—Quality of Glasses necessary for Ambrotypes... 125

CHAPTER IX.

Apparatus for Ambrotypes—Chemicals used—Substances for finishing the Picture—Preparation of the Nitrate Bath—To Iodize the Bath—Filtering Process—Adding Acid—Neutralizing the Bath—Full Directions for keeping the Bath in order—Renewal of the Nitrate of Silver 131

CHAPTER X.

The Developing Solutions—Manner of Compounding them—Various Formulæ for Developing Solutions—Test of Acetic Acid—The Fixing Solutions—Cyanide of Potassium—Hyposulphite of Soda—Adding Chloride of Silver....... 141

CHAPTER XI.

On the Practice of the Art in all its Details, from the Cleaning of the Plate to the Application of the Fixing Solution—Drying the Picture 145

CHAPTER XII.

Varnishing the Picture—Single Glass Process—Stereoscopic Ambrotype—Treble Glass Process—The Double Glass Process—Cutting's Patent—The Patent-leather Process................... 151

CHAPTER XIII.

The Manufacture of Gun-Cotton—Test of the Acids employed—Washing and Drying the Gun-Cotton—Preparation of the Collodion—Its Nature and Properties—Ether and Alcohol—To Iodize Collodion for Ambrotypes—Method of preserving Collodion, and keeping it ready for use—Tests of good Collodion—To remove the color from Collodion 157

CHAPTER XIV.

Coloring Ambrotypes—Colors employed—Ambrotypes for Lockets—Taking Views—Copying Daguerreotypes by the Ambrotype Process—Copying Engravings, Statuary, Machinery, &c..... 166

CHAPTER XV.

On the manner of Arranging the Light—The Falling of the same on the Drapery—Use of a Diaphragm—Light on the Eyes—Using Screens—Backgrounds—Reflectors—Diaphragm—Time in the Camera—Over-exposure, and Under-developing—Taking Children's Portraits.. 174

CHAPTER XVI.

Alcoholic Solutions for preparing Collodion—Iodide of Silver Solution—Bromide of Silver Solution—Bromo-Iodide of Silver Solution—Saturated Solution of Iodide of Potassium in Alcohol—Of Bromide of Potassium—To make Hydro-bromic Acid....... 179

CONTENTS. 13

CHAPTER XVII.

Preparation of the Varnishes—White Copal Varnish—Gum-demar Varnish—Black Asphaltum Varnish—White Varnish of Shellac and Copal—Thickened Varnish for Cementing Glasses, in place of Canada Balsam—Gum-shellac Varnish for Plate-holders—Applying the Varnishes 189

CHAPTER XVIII.

Causes of Failure in the Practice of the Art—Fogging the Pictures—To detect the Fogging of Plates—Black and White Specks on the Plates—Transparent and Opaque Spots—Impurity of Chemicals—Spots or Streaks on the Glass Plates.................. 194

CHAPTER XIX.

Cautions with regard to using the various Chemical Substances in making Gun-Cotton—Use of Ether and Alcohol—Use of Cyanide of Potassium—Nitrate of Silver—Cleaning the Hands—Solution for cleaning the Hands—Hints on the various Processes connected with Positives and Negatives—To render Collodion highly Sensitive—The Lampratype Process 202

CHAPTER XX.

Vocabulary of Photographic Chemicals—Acetic Acid—Alcohol—Ammonia—Bromine—Bromide of Potassium—Carbonate of Soda—Cyanide of Potassium—Chloride of Gold—Hyposulphite of Gold—Hyposulphite of Soda—Iodine—Iodide of Ammonia—Iodide of Potassium—Iodide of Silver—Protosulphate of Iron—Litmus—Nitric Acid—Nitrate of Potash—Nitrate of Silver—Sulphuric Acid—Properties of Ether—Properties of Water..... 211

WEIGHTS AND MEASURES 233

INTRODUCTION

TO

THE AMBROTYPE MANUAL.

The Photographic Art, as known and practised at the present time, is capable of a great variety of modifications. Among these are positive pictures on glass, which, on account of their imperishability, are denominated Ambrotypes—a name given to them by Mr. Cutting, a successful artist of Boston. They are said to be impervious either to air or water.

It is by this name that all positive pictures on glass are known in this country. They are attracting the attention of the Daguerreian artists from the peculiarity of their appearance, and the new phenomena of their production, differing so widely from the Daguerreotype process.

A desire has been often expressed that a work written by a practical operator, and of a practical nature, might be within the reach of those who wish either to begin the study of the art at the outset, or to modify and improve the practice in which they may be already engaged. With a view to meet this want, the present work has been undertaken.

It is designed to present the results of a long practical experience, and of a uniform series of experiments in all the details of the art, together with receipts by the most skilful and successful operators of the present day.

Ambrotypes being positive photographs on glass, it will necessarily require some knowledge of photography to fully understand the so-called ambrotype process.

In this manual will be found such practical hints on the various processes (divested, as much as possible, of technical expressions, which may tend to mislead the inexperienced artist), as, with a little practice under the supervision of one who has some knowledge of manipulating, will enable any person to master the art.

The patented process known as "Cutting's Patent" has tended in some measure to retard the efforts of many who were desirous to work by this process. At present, however, certain investigations are being made so as to undeceive the public on this point, and we can see the good results of a removal of this drawback to the successful practice of this beautiful art. There are various other methods of sealing the ambrotypes which will answer as well as those indicated in the patented process, if not better, which no one need be deterred from adopting.

In this work will be found detailed the many various processes which have been adopted by skilful artists. The whole operation from the first cleaning of the glass plate to the final sealing of the picture will be elucidated and explained in such a clear and satisfactory manner, as that it may be hoped that the amateur may make great proficiency in his practice after the perusal of the work.

The process, however, is capable of such a variety of changes, all tending to the same result, and liable, also, to a slight variation, without due care, that many, perhaps, who may adopt the practice will meet with difficulties where none were expected. But perseverance, which accomplishes great deeds in all things, will at length reward the industrious student in this almost magic field of science. We believe that the day is not far distant when ambrotypes will be classed among the most beautiful creations of the Photographic Art, and command the wonder and regard of the picture-loving public.

The art is capable of much greater variety of effects than the long-practised Daguerreotype. Here we may seal a picture with or without coloring, and make the same picture appear to be colored on viewing it on one side, and uncolored on viewing it on the other side—in truth, viewing two sides of the face with only one portrait. Added to which is the great reduction of the time in the camera, by which *moving objects* and *views* may be taken without reversing, and likenesses of young children can be indelibly fixed on the glass tablet.

For the production of groups, this process offers many facilities not possessed by any other, from the fact that the ordinary iron head-rests may be dispensed with, if desirable, and an easy, graceful, and natural position attained.

These and other considerations render the Ambrotype in many respects superior to other photographic processes, and it will deservedly command the attention of all artists who wish to excel in this profession.

PHOTOGRAPHY.

CHAPTER I.

HISTORY AND PROGRESS OF THE PHOTOGRAPHIC ART—ITS INTRODUCTION INTO THE UNITED STATES—THE DISCOVERY OR USES OF THE VARIOUS CHEMICALS—POSITIVE PHOTOGRAPHS ON GLASS.

The history and progress of an art so peculiarly distinct from all other arts, demands from its votaries a certain knowledge of its early stages, its introduction to the world, and its authors who brought it into being.

The names of many of those who have been instrumental in perfecting it, are fast passing away, and it seems befitting that, if only as a tribute of respect to their memories, some mention at least should be made of their noble achievements in this field of science—especially their long and wearisome researches and labors in perfecting this wonderful work.

To M. Daguerre, of France, whose name is so

identified with the Photographic Art, from the fact of its being associated with all those impressions on the metallic plate, is the world not only indebted for the first sublime idea, but also the first successful result. Although Mr. Fox Talbot, of England, who was prosecuting experiments at the same time with Daguerre, claims priority of discovery, yet the world would have slumbered in ignorance had not M. Daguerre so clearly demonstrated that light falling upon a certain substance known by chemists as iodide of silver, would impress thereon whatever image was presented for its magic work, and reproduce its own image with all the fidelity of an artist's skill.

The details of M. Daguerre's process, as given to the world in June, 1839, were, of course, very imperfect; yet the principle was thereby established, and has been so successfully carried out by his successors, that he is fully entitled to the credit, and deservedly stands pre-eminent in the ranks as the original discoverer or inventor of this beautiful art.

All the photographic processes since made known and practised, owe their origin, if not directly, at least indirectly, to the fact of his original discovery.

Pictures on paper, glass, &c., are in fact only modifications of his great achievement. They involve a change in the nature of the mere materials used, and do not in any degree affect the original fact that light must be brought to act upon the substance known as iodide of silver to produce the required result.

The researches of Wedgewood and Sir Humphrey Davy, in 1802, are familiar to most scientific readers. These individuals were cognizant of the fact that light acting upon certain salts of silver affected its color. They engaged in these experiments in order to fix the image in the camera obscura at that early day; yet owing to the imperfect state of chemical science, and the fact that iodine itself was not discovered at that time, they finally abandoned it, and left the field for such industrious and worthy investigators as Daguerre and Niepce, who successfully prosecuted their researches, beginning in 1814, and finally announcing their successful result in June, 1839.

The world was astounded to be told that the seeming evanescent image that had flitted so beautifully before the vision of a dreamer's mind in the camera obscura for so many long years, had been caught and impressed indelibly upon a tangible substance; that the long wished-for aspirations of an artist's soul had been realized; that now it was possible to transform the living pictures which Portia, two hundred years before, had exhibited to the gazing world as wonders of his genius; that they could all be imperishably impressed, and be made to retain their beauty for ages.

Philosophers' in science prosecuted their researches, and finally made additional discoveries. We find Sir John Herschel as among the foremost in the ranks. Hunt, Archer, and Mr. Fox Talbot himself, made great progress soon after it was announced that Daguerre had finally perfected his discovery.

Mr. Talbot, however, was unwilling the world itself should profit by his discovery, and he forthwith commissioned agents to all parts of the world to secure patents wherever they could be obtained. With what success he met in their sale may be known from the fact that no one now claims any interest whatever in them.

Mr. Talbot has seen proper of late to withdraw all claims to a patent by his process, and for the reason, no doubt, that it has been so immeasurably superseded by new and more useful improvements.

A patent for any portion of this process is almost

conceded to be a misnomer. Certain it is that one always militates against the successful practice of it; and had M. Daguerre claimed one all over the world, his name would not have attained its present fame.

Mr. Talbot has been very justly censured in England for his long persistency in the claims to his patent. Many litigations were the consequences of it, in all of which Mr. Talbot was not declared the victor, but he always brought upon himself the deserved censure of the photographers in Europe.

M. Daguerre himself, very reluctantly, however, yielded to the wishes of some of his friends, and secured a patent in England, by taking advantage of a peculiarity in the patent laws of that country, yet it has been said he often regretted it.

Wherever any patent has been secured for any peculiar detail of the Photographic Art, it has always tended to bring discredit on its projectors, and render them odious in the eyes of the fraternity, as grasping and over-reaching in their endeavors to gain a few dollars and cents out of this beautiful process, which seems to belong to a higher race of discoveries than most others, partaking almost of the things spiritual.

France awarded M. Daguerre a pension for life, as well as one to M. Niepce, *junior*, the father, who was the original co-laborer with Daguerre, having died in 1833. This pension was small, yet it evinced a noble and generous spirit in the French government, and an example that is worthy of emulation in other countries.

The process on silver plates soon made rapid strides towards perfection, and in a few years we find the art capable of producing specimens of great beauty. The discovery of the use of chloride of iodine, and bromine, and finally the gilding process of Mr. Fizeau, resulted successfully in completing the whole process so perfectly, that few, if any, material improvements have been made since.

This led others to investigate and essay experiments on various substances instead of the silver plate, that being an expensive article; and, moreover, as the daguerreotype could only be seen with distinctness in a certain position, or angle of light, while paper offered such unequal surfaces, a natural desire was expressed to find some other substance to remedy these defects. This first led Sir John Herschel to adopt glass as the readiest means of obviating the difficulties. This was in the year 1844, and he obtained his results by precipitating iodine and bromine, and chloride of silver upon glass. With this he produced some good negatives, which could be converted into excellent positives.

Herschel describes his process as follows: "The glass plate so prepared receives in the camera a distinct negative image, which appears either in a natural position, or reversed, as you look at it in front or behind. If a solution of hyposulphite of soda is spread cautiously over the surface, and the latter is afterwards rinsed with water, the picture vanishes, but as soon as the plate is dry, it comes again to light, when it looks similar in appearance to a daguerreotype, more especially if it is placed on a dark ground, or blackened over the lamp, whereby, indeed, the negative is made positive."

Here, then, we have the first germ of a positive picture on glass. Herschel himself was searching after a negative picture whereby to produce a positive on paper, nor did it occur to him to produce a positive on glass. Had he done so, then the far-famed Ambrotypes, or positive photographs on glass, would have been of an earlier creation than those of 1850 in England.

We see here the actual beginning of this art as far back as 1844.

The next improvement was made by Niepce de St. Victor, of France, in 1848, which consisted in the use of albumen (the white of an egg), containing iodine and a small portion of water. This was used for coating glass plates, and was practised with good success. It was found to possess only a small degree of sensitiveness. Yet it has been since used for taking views, having a further combination of bromine, with excellent results. M. Le Grey, of Paris, was the first to suggest the use of waxed paper. This process, with albumen, gives highly satisfactory pictures, and is only excelled by the use of collodion. It was in 1850 that tha' substance first was known as the great desideratum of the Photographic Art, and from its discovery and foundation has been laid a superstructure which commands so much admiration in the scientific world.

Had not Professor Schönbein, of Basle, Switzerland, in 1846, made that curious, and at that time almost useless, discovery of gun-cotton, we should have groped our way in darkness in search of a substance that would render all our labors so sure of success.

The use of gun-cotton as an explosive material instead of gunpowder, was by some predicted when its discovery was first made known; but it was soon found to be useless as an explosive agent, when happily a new element of its nature was developed in the fact of its solubility in ether or alcohol. This produced the substance known as collodion, from a Greek word signifying "to stick." Its similarity to albumen soon caused it to be used instead of that substance, when lo! a servant was obtained for the photographic artist at once so useful and willing that he has ever since, and probably ever will, be subject to his rule.

Collodion was first used in 1850, several claiming the origin of the discovery. Amongst the number may be mentioned Messrs. Archer, Fry, and Diamond, of London, together with Le Grey, of Paris, and De La Motte. The latter asserts that M. Simon, an apothecary of Berlin, suggested its properties to him in the spring of 1850.

After collodion had been established as a photographic agent of such vast utility, it was soon found that positive pictures could be taken on glass with greater facility than those on the silver plate, and we find that many were sold in 1851 in that manner in England; yet they did not command much attention, owing to their peculiar nature—being taken with a thin film, and a weak nitrate bath, they did not possess that strength which those of the present day exhibit.

The use of collodion was employed mainly with a view to produce good negatives on glass, in order to obtain from them satisfactory positives on paper. It was not until positive pictures on glass were taken in this country, that they elicited any praise from the artist; and we find Mr. Cutting, of Boston, running with railroad speed towards the Patent Office in Washington, and securing the exclusive privilege of sealing two glasses, with one of them blackened, in order to render the picture apparent—the examiners at Washington not dreaming of the capital joke which was being played on them, for it is well known that these positives cannot be seen without the black varnish.

The necessity of the second glass blackened has since been entirely obviated by applying the varnish directly to the picture, and at the same time rendering the picture more durable, by entirely excluding from it the air or dust.

Since that patent was obtained, there have been many improvements made in the preparation of the chemicals, and their use, all of which have entirely superseded those of Mr. Cutting's, whose chemicals, strange to say, were also patented.

The name of Ambrotype was also given them, and they are now so well known by it, that it is presumed they will be ever after called by that newly-coined word, which of itself is perhaps as suggestive and appropriate as any.

Thus we see the progress of photographs on glass has resulted in establishing an entirely new name for pictures which owe their origin to the immortal Daguerre. And although many of the followers of the great master in the art claim originality in many of the details of this art, and they are indeed entitled to much praise, yet had Daguerre and Niepce never lived, this art might not yet have had an existence. But Daguerre developed and perfected an art which will be practised as long as the sun shall shine.

CHAPTER II.

THEORY OF THE PHOTOGRAPHIC PROCESS—NEGATIVE AND POSITIVE PICTURES—NEGATIVES ON PAPER AND ON GLASS—POSITIVES ON GLASS—THEORY OF THE POSITIVE AND THE NEGATIVE PROCESS.

The photographic process is one of the latest arts introduced to the world which partakes, in some degree, of the arts of design, and from its nature is really superior, in point of attractive features, to many of the lesser arts. It seems to demand a more elevated range of thought and taste than others, being to a great degree allied to the arts of painting and sculpture. Though in a measure mechanical, yet it possesses many peculiarities which demand from its votaries more than the limited judgment and skill necessary to the perfection of ordinary arts.

The theory of the process is said mainly to consist in that *certain action* to which light is subject of causing its own image or reflection to be rendered apparent by that self-same reflection on substances capable of receiving the impression.

The term Photography, or *painting by light*, is sufficiently definite for our purpose, and all we know about the actual theory is, that when certain conditions are observed with regard to light, an impression may be obtained. But what is the real or definite action which takes place upon the surface of the iodized plate, no man has been permitted to know.

Photographs are known either as Negatives or Positives. They are positive in the Daguerreotype and Ambrotype, and negative only in the glass pictures or paper pictures, from which positives are to be taken on paper, and on other similar substances. These terms should be well understood by the operator who seeks success, as they form the basis of all photography.

All pictures taken by the collodion process possess either of the foregoing conditions.

Negatives were first taken on paper, from which positives were produced by the process known as the Calotype, discovered and patented by Mr. Fox Talbot, of England. From the multiplicity of its imperfections, it did not succeed, and no photographs were appreciated by a discerning public until those negatives taken on glass were produced and positives exhibited from them which were creditable as works of art.

Negatives possess all the various phenomena in their production that are possessed by positives. They are in some respects more difficult to be obtained in great perfection, and in others are less so from their peculiar properties. They are, in fact, only matrixes from which other pictures can be obtained. Therefore they are not perfect pictures of themselves, but only parts of a whole.

The manipulation connected with the negative process is given briefly in this work, mainly with a view to impart certain information with regard to the positive process.

The theory of the positive and negative processes is the same, which consists in the reduction of the silver to an oxide on the surface of the glass by the action of light, and the subsequent application of well-known chemical substances. These several conditions must be well observed in order to secure good results. The iodide of silver must be well formed on the surface of the glass. The light given must be only so much as will produce the image, and reveal it after the application of the developing solution, and this must be of just the requisite strength to produce the reduction from the iodide to the oxide of silver.

The impression is therefore given solely by the action of light, or by certain properties of that mysterious body. Yet when the plate is removed from the camera, there is no apparent change produced, but on applying the developing solution, the sleeping and invisible image awakes and starts into life, and commands from every beholder an expression of wonder and admiration.

Fixing the picture is a subsequent operation, and is no part of the process of production, only so far as it may be necessary to render it permanent, and also to remove the unaffected iodide of silver, a portion of which is not at all changed by the light. Only those parts are affected which are necessary to produce the light and shade.

Positives on glass are taken with chemicals varying slightly from those used in producing negatives, and also by a much shorter exposure in the camera. In fact, a positive is only a negative with a less degree of exposure to the action of light. All positives could of themselves become negatives were the time of exposure prolonged sufficiently to effect that result, though their use as a means of producing subsequent positives on paper is a matter of doubt, for there are certain other conditions necessary for success in the production of good negatives not known in the positive process.

These positives on glass are now so widely recognized as *Ambrotypes,* that we shall venture to assume that name as one sufficiently significant and appropriate for our purpose.

Ambrotypes are now so well known, that they may almost be said to be identified with the progress of the art in the United States, and belong exclusively to this country. They are not known as such in Europe. They are there classed under the head of Photographs, and the public here are frequently led into error on this point, and suppose, in fact, that Ambrotypes are a new creation —a new kind of picture only known here, while in truth they were first taken in Europe, and are merely photographs on glass, taken positively instead of negatively.

The details of the process, and the necessary manipulations, are of course to be found only in the practical portion of this work.

The whole art consists, therefore, in the careful preparation of the glass plate, in the most scrupulous cleanliness and accuracy of the employment of every material requisite to the process, and in a most implicit obedience to such rules as are laid down in this work for the guidance of those who would insure success.

The results set forth in these pages were obtained after much patient labor and investigation on the part of a host of intelligent inquirers, who have successfully overcome difficulties which, could they have foreseen, would have appalled the most patient and determined mind. Happily for the photographer who now commences his operations, he may profit by the experience of others, and be spared the labor and investigation of earlier operators.

The path for him is now rid of its most formidable difficulties, and should he be induced to examine carefully the abstruse philosophical principles upon which this fascinating art depends, he may, in his turn, become a contributor to its improvement and advancement.

The experience of the humblest may sometimes furnish a suggestion, which investigations of the most refined and cultivated may have long failed to accomplish.

The art is greatly suggestive. It offers many fields of speculation, and the great aim of all who practise it should be to perfect it as soon as possible, for, like all the creations of man's genius, it is not yet complete. But the rapid strides it is now making towards long wished-for perfection are so apparent, that we confidently look to the accomplishment of the greatest end sought—namely, the reproduction of the *colors of nature*. This result once obtained, the artist could lay aside his easel and pallet. He could then retire from the arena where he now stands contending so unprofitably, in a pecuniary point of view, with the photographer.

But this seeming triumph of nature over art by the pencillings of the sunlight—the sun himself becoming the universal and sublime artist!—is really the triumph of art over nature; for since art, conscious of the weakness and imperfections of her best efforts, has had the tact and skill to wheel the forces of nature into her own ranks, the result should be set down to her own credit, as her own victory.

PART I.

PRACTICAL DETAILS

OF THE

NEGATIVE PROCESS.

POSITIVE PHOTOGRAPHS ON PAPER.

CHAPTER I.

ON THE PRACTICE OF THE NEGATIVE PROCESS THROUGH ALL ITS DETAILS—THE MANIPULATIONS—CLEANING THE PLATE—COATING WITH COLLODION—DRYING THE SAME—TIME IN THE CAMERA—DEVELOPING—RE-DEVELOPING FOR INTENSITY—VARNISHING THE NEGATIVE—FRAMES OR SHELVES FOR NEGATIVES—GENERAL REMARKS ON THE MANIPULATION OF THE NEGATIVE PROCESS—ARRANGEMENT OF THE LIGHT—USE OF THE CAMERA, ETC., ETC.

There are so many various plans suggested by practical operators in the Photographic Art, all varying so much in detail, that the author has thought proper to simply confine himself to one line of practice, which has been found to produce the best results.

All negative Photographs at the present stage

of the art are taken on glass, and they are called negatives from the fact that all the lights and shades are reversed—*i. e.* where the portrait in life presents the high lights (or where the light falls the strongest, and it should appear the lightest), in the negative it appears the darkest. In like manner, where the dark shades are seen in a positive to be dark as in life, in the negative they are seen light, or to present the high lights. They present these peculiar phenomena only when viewed by transmitted light, or light passing through them, in which position they can only be seen with proper effect. When viewed as a positive, laid on a blackened substance, they resemble in some degree a positive that has been too long exposed in the camera. They cannot be viewed properly in any other manner than by transmitted light.

However, they are never to be sealed up for sale in any form, but are always reserved by the artist to print from, any number of copies that may be desired. And herein consists the great beauty and perfection of this branch of photography. We have the power of multiplying *ad infinitum*, even far greater than if it were printed from an engraving. The negative itself can be reproduced and multiplied so that exact *fac-similes* could be obtained, and even thousands printed by every negative, so nearly resembling each other, that none could distinguish the first original positive impression.

Regarding the manipulation of negative process as a simple chemical operation, with certain chemical auxiliaries, it is very easy of accomplishment. When once properly understood, if certain rules are observed, it is more sure of success than most others in the art.

The first requisite to success is the cleaning of the glass plate, which is easily done by rubbing it with a piece of cotton-flannel dipped in alcohol, slightly diluted with water; and in case of using the glass the second time, a small quantity of rotten-stone, whiting, or tripoli powder, may be added.

Be careful to dust the glass with a flat camel's-hair brush just before pouring on the collodion. Holding the glass in the left hand, standing near the bath, pour the collodion on with a continuous stream from the bottle until there is enough, which when flowed over the whole surface of the glass will just cover it. Then let the superfluous quantity run off at the right-hand corner into the bottle, slightly moving the glass plate so that the collodion will not dry in lines or ridges; a quick motion may be necessary to insure a perfect flow of it over the surface. On holding the glass up to transmitted light, it should appear perfectly clear and transparent, as though no collodion was upon its surface—at least, no lines, streaks, or spots. If any are visible, the negative will be faulty.

Let it dry until it appears almost free from moisture; now darken the room; then place it in the bath for one or two minutes, or until the iodide of silver is perfectly formed on its surface, which can easily be ascertained by raising the plate from the bath. If the surface presents a uniform appearance, clear and without any lines or streaks like grease or oil, then it is ready for the camera: a slight motion of the plate will produce this result.

The time of exposure in the camera is entirely a matter of judgment and experience. No definite rules can be laid down; but usually, in a strong light, with the ammonia collodion and the neutral bath, from fifteen seconds to one minute will answer.

The time of exposure can easily be ascertained by a trial plate.

THE DEVELOPING OF THE NEGATIVE.

This requires great care and much practice, for if the process in all its details is correctly followed, and only a slight variation in the developing of the image, the resulting negative will be of no avail.

As soon as possible after the light has acted upon the plate in the camera, remove it to the developing-stand, or it may be held in the hand, and pour the solution well filtered upon the surface, but only just enough to cover it, retaining all the free nitrate of silver which had adhered to the plate on its removal from the bath. The silver itself acts as a means of darkening the negative.

The developing solution of protosulphite of iron, on page 89, will be found the most useful, and indeed the only one recommended for good negatives. After allowing this solution to remain on the surface for a few seconds, the outlines of the negative will appear. Then, if not sufficiently intense, pour off the developer, and cover it again two or three times, until sufficient intensity is obtained. The negative should gradually appear first in the high light, then the drapery; and, lastly, it should seem to fade partially away.

FIXING THE NEGATIVE.

Always fix the negative in a strong solution of hyposulphite of soda. This will of course remove the iodide of silver slowly, but the collodion is less liable to be attacked by the use of soda than by cyanide of potassium. A saturated solution will remove the iodide of silver more readily, although a less quantity of soda will answer. It is found that whatever quantity is employed, it loses its strength on the immersion of every plate, and must be frequently renewed.

VARNISHING NEGATIVES.

In order to preserve negatives in a proper state for future use, it is well to varnish them. If they are intended only to print a few copies, a varnish of gum-arabic is preferable, not very thick, about the consistency of collodion.

If the negative is required for many prints, the better course would be to varnish with the white negative varnish. All varnishes are poured over the plate in the same manner as collodion, and allowed to dry by being placed on its edge, secure from dust, until it has thoroughly dried.

FRAMES OR SHELVES FOR HOLDING NEGATIVES.

It is very necessary that the negatives should be kept in some secure place; and two shelves, having grooves in them above and below, so that the glasses shall stand on the edges in them, is the best receptacle when not in use. Shelves of various widths, according to the size of the glasses, are required, and with a door that shall close in front of each to exclude the dust, &c.

The manipulation of the negative process is so very important, that certain hints are necessary to insure absolute success.

The arrangement of the light upon the sitter is of vast importance. It should fall with a full force upon the drapery, if it is of a dark color; and the background, which is usually of a somber hue, should also be well lighted up from the skylight. Arrange the subject in a favorable position to produce the most pleasing effect of light and shade upon the face—carefully attending to the pointed light upon the eyes. Avoid the long line of light upon them. If possible, produce a uniform light on the drapery, as that portion is more likely to be clouded than any other.

The position of the camera should demand a

careful study. Some cameras require to be elevated more than others, which can be ascertained by actual experiment. Some will work more uniformly over the whole plate when arranged in an exact line with the face of the sitter.

A skylight which is nearly flat, or one that is slightly elevated only on one side, has been found to produce the most pleasing effects in Photography.

The length of time of exposure of the plate to the action of light is a matter of vast importance, because the intensity of the negative is affected thereby—which will be seen on application of the developing agent. If too long time has been employed, the print will appear flat in details; although the drapery may appear distinct, the roundness will be lost. The middle tints of the face which are so desirable, will not appear. It is better to give a short time first, and bring up the intensity by developing. A short exposure in the camera, if the developing solutions are capable of producing a powerful negative, is found to be the best for strong and vigorous effects. The point to arrive at is to allow just long enough exposure that the developing agent shall just bring out the negative of the required intensity, and no more.

By a trial picture giving what may be supposed nearly the exact time, if too short the augmentation of the next succeeding trials will eventually arrive at the correct result.

It may be proper to mention, that glasses used for negatives do not require to be of such purity as those designed for positives; even good window-glass, which is selected as free from bubbles as possible, will answer a very good purpose. The expense, therefore, for material for Photographic negatives will not be very great, and the artist can retain them for future use after one or two impressions have been taken, so that any future day he may produce more pictures for his patron without any additional sitting.

CHAPTER II.

THE NITRATE OF SILVER BATH FOR NEGATIVES—PREPARATION OF THE SAME—FORMATION OF THE IODIDE OF SILVER FOR THE NITRATE BATH—ON THE PRACTICE OF THE NEGATIVE BATH—OBSERVATIONS ON THE USE OF THE NEGATIVE BATH—ON THE INTENSITY OF THE NEGATIVE—COLOR OF THE NEGATIVE, ETC., ETC.

THE NITRATE OF SILVER BATH FOR NEGATIVES.

The bath of nitrate of silver, which is most commonly in use for negatives, is that known as the nitrate bath. Great care is essential to its proper preparation, and we shall proceed to lay down the precise form to make a bath that will produce the most satisfactory results. The proportion of nitrate of silver required to each ounce of water is usually about fifty grains, though this is not absolutely essential.

All negative baths require a certain degree of working or use before they will act to the best ad-

THE NITRATE OF SILVER BATH. 49

vantage. They should always be combined with a portion of iodide of silver; and even that should be added again after long use, as many times that simple remedy will remove difficulties which were deemed insurmountable.

Having ascertained the number of ounces the bath contains (see page 50), weigh out the quantity of nitrate of silver necessary to produce, when dissolved, about fifty grains to each ounce of water. Dissolve about one ounce of the nitrate of silver in four or six ounces of water; then dissolve the balance of the nitrate of silver which will be required to fill the bath in the remaining portion of the water.

For every ounce of nitrate of silver which is required in the bath to render it fifty grains to each ounce of water, there must be measured out three grains of iodide of ammonia. This is to be formed into iodide of silver by first dissolving the iodide of ammonia in about two ounces of water, and adding thereto say two fluid drachms of the solution of nitrate of silver, in which one ounce of the silver has been dissolved in four ounces of water. This will immediately throw down a yellow precipitate, which is the iodide of silver. Wash this precipitate three times with water, by filling the graduate dish or bottle, which should contain at least six ounces of water, and allow it to settle; then pour off the water, leaving the iodide of silver at the bottom. When this is well washed, add it to the ounce of silver previously dissolved in the four ounces of water. Shake it well, then pour the whole into the bottle containing the bath. A milky appearance will be seen in the bath, which is well to remain in that state for a few hours to dissolve as much of the iodide of silver as possible. After filtering the bath until it becomes clear, it is ready for use.

A bath prepared according to the foregoing, if required to be of sixty-four ounces of water, would contain the following proportions:

$64 \times 50 = 3200$ grains, or of nitrate of silver $6\frac{3}{4}$ ounces.
Iodide of ammonia . . . . . 20 grains.
Water . . . . 2 quarts.

There will be in $6\frac{3}{4}$ ounces of silver, 3240 grains, allowing 480 grains to each ounce. The above quantity will be as near 50 grains to the ounce as will be required for all practical purposes.

Distilled water is preferable in all cases. Though perfectly pure, soft water will answer, if it has not been kept long in wooden vessels. If it has been so kept, it can be first boiled and filtered through paper, to remove any traces of vegetable matters.

By referring to pp. 133 and 134, and the subsequent pages relating to the preparation of the nitrate of silver bath for Ambrotypes, much valuable information will be found, which can be adopted in the negative bath. The bath will require neutralizing, should any excess of acid accrue in it. The process of neutralizing will be found on page 137.

The negative collodion, which is more frequently used with a perfectly neutral bath, as above described, is that recipe found on page 82.

ON THE PRACTICE OF THE NEGATIVE BATH.

The use of the negative bath requires much care and attention, for herein lies one of the elements of success in the production of perfect negative impressions.

By using the ammonia collodion constantly, the bath is liable to be changed, as it necessarily must be, in its chemical character. Iodide of silver is formed upon each plate, and consequently less silver is contained in the solution, and alcohol is added to the compound from the collodion, as well as a trace of ether. It will soon be found to be slightly acid in testing with litmus-paper. This acid tendency sometimes is not objectionable; but if there is too much of it, neutralize the bath, and test with a hydrometer to ascertain the strength of silver. Always keep the strength equal to fifty grains to the ounce. In adding more silver to the bath, it may be effected more readily by first dissolving the quantity required in a separate bottle from the one used expressly for the nitrate bath. Filter always before adding to the bath. Always be provided with two bottles, having glass stoppers sufficiently large to hold the contents of the nitrate bath, into one of which it may be filtered.

It is recommended also to add silver often to the bath, if it is in constant use, because if the greater portion of the solution is removed (as some must necessarily be every time a plate is immersed) by adding a large quantity, the whole nature of the bath is changed.

Many operators provide themselves with sufficient solutions for two or three baths. This is a plan highly recommended, as a bath actually improves by age, even if it is not worked every day. Old baths which have been laid aside as useless except for restoration, have, after many days, on a new trial been found to produce good results.

There is a constant change taking place in the nitrate baths, and there are many phenomena connected with them wholly unexplained as yet by the most successful operators. Sometimes an acid bath will work more surely for negatives than a neutral, and sometimes a neutral bath is preferred. The general rule to be observed is, that, if a bath is acid, the time of exposure in the camera is lengthened, and as we approach the neutral point the time is lessened. Therefore to work a bath as nearly neutral as possible, is the most sure of success.

In order that the negatives should produce good positive pictures on paper, they should be very transparent in the dark portions, such as the drapery, &c., and of such intensity in the light parts that a ray of light can with difficulty be transmitted, and this must be combined with a regular gradation in the middle tints.

These desirable results can be attained by using the collodion somewhat thicker for the negatives than for positives or Ambrotypes, as thereby a thicker deposit of silver is obtained on the surface of the glass.

Also a stronger nitrate bath, and using it as nearly neutral as possible, and a longer exposure in the camera, together with less acid in the developer; all these combined will produce the desired end, viz., an intensity such as will print positives having all the beauty so much desired in good Photographs. The absolute intensity, however, of a negative does not always depend upon the thickness of metallic silver, but to a certain extent upon the color it may have when seen by transmitted light. Negatives also vary in color; some are translucent and of a bronze color, others are of a bluish-black, whilst some are of a gray color. The color most to be sought after is the bluish-black, because these are found to print more uniformly clear in their details.

Sometimes the best negatives are those which may appear to be weak, because the chemical rays are more obstructed, and the print is consequently more uniform in its gradations of light and shade.

The color of the negatives depends on certain conditions of the bath, the time of exposure in the camera, the nature and strength of the developer, and the quantity of acetic acid contained in it. Sometimes the presence of organic matter, which will collect in the bath, may affect the color and tone of the negatives. So that no positive rules can be laid down for the continued action of a bath; practice alone must be the teacher in this branch of the art.

Seeming uncertainties may appear to some who have not had much experience in the art as obstacles of great moment. But they will all vanish after a short time. These apparent contradictions and perplexities are only met with for any length of time in the experience of those persons who do not attend to the minute details of the art, such as cleaning well the plate, decanting the collodion, the proper length of time of developing the picture, &c. The practice of this beautiful art must not be condemned because it contains a few seeming contradictions; for if it was easily acquired, and always certain of success, there would be no incentive to excellence, and those persons who possessed only a limited taste and experience, could rival the artist in the creations of his genius. It may therefore be deemed a fortunate circumstance to those who would wish to excel, that the road to full success lays through a few rugged passes, and he who would reach the goal of perfect accomplishment must encounter some difficulties.

CHAPTER III.

ON PHOTOGRAPHIC PRINTING—SALTING SOLUTIONS—SALTING THE PAPER—SILVERING THE PAPER WITH AMMONIA NITRATE OF SILVER—PLAIN SILVER SOLUTION—TO PREPARE THE ALBUMEN FOR PAPER POSITIVES—SILVERING ALBUMEN PAPER—ON THE PRACTICE OF PRINTING NEGATIVES—TONING OR FIXING THE PRINT—WASHING THE POSITIVE PRINTS—DRYING THE PICTURES—VARNISHING AND MOUNTING THE PRINTS.

The printing of the Photographs is that portion of the art wherein great care and attention is demanded, and where much of the beauty and finish of the picture is due. The success of it depends upon a perfectly proper understanding of the process.

Having selected the best quality of paper, it may for convenience be cut into sizes such as will be required for use in the printing frames. Though this is not absolutely necessary, the large sheets, as they are manufactured and imported for use, can first be salted, dried, and laid aside in some secure place, free from dust or fumes of chemicals. When wanted for use, they may be cut of whatever size may be required.

THE SALTING SOLUTIONS.

One quart of pure soft water.

90 grains of hydrochlorate of ammonia, or common sal ammoniac.

(Sal ammoniac is found to be the best preparation of salt, as it contains less impurities than any other known.)

Dissolve and filter.

Place this in a large flat dish, which may be of gutta-percha, earthenware, or porcelain, or even wood, if it is varnished thoroughly with gum-shellac varnish. The dish must be nearly filled, and of sufficient dimensions to admit the whole sheet of paper if laid in it.

The paper is to be immersed one sheet at a time, by laying hold of the sheet at two corners, and it must be drawn quickly through the solution twice, allowing the liquid to wet it as it may on the surface of the paper only, in effect to lay the solution of salt upon its surface without disturbing the fibres of the paper.

Hang each sheet up separately to dry in a room free from dust or any chemical exhalations. The better plan of suspending paper, either in the salting or silvering process, is to use the patent clothes-pins, which can be arranged on a cord across the room. Great care should be observed in salting the paper to avoid stains, spots, or wrinkles. The hands should never touch any portion of the paper except the corners. The salted papers can be laid aside, and will keep for a great length of time.

SILVERING THE PAPER.

The paper already salted and dried, to be silvered, may be effected by two or three methods.

The ammonia nitrate solution, the preparation of which is described on page 95, is the one mostly in use, and one that will produce, with plain salted paper, the most pleasing results.

The silver solution which may be required for use at one time, is first filtered into a clean bottle, and the paper laid upon a flat surface, covered with paper or card-board, is to be fastened down by the corners with pins or any other article which will cause it to remain stationary. The silver solution is then poured on the middle of the paper, enough to cover it; and with a ball of cotton just newly prepared, carefully spread the silver over the whole surface, by means of round lines or circles, from the centre of the paper to the circumference. The superfluous silver can be poured into a bottle, but not used again, as it is changed into a chloride of silver, owing to its contact with the salt of the paper. It may be reserved in the bottle, to mix with other silver solutions, that are useless except for the restoration of the pure silver, as described on page 105. The same ball of cotton can be employed to silver all the papers that may be wanted at one time, if it is laid on a clean piece of paper, but a new one will be required for a subsequent preparation.

The silvered papers should be hung up to dry in a dark room, and only enough prepared that may be wanted for immediate use. In the winter season, however, they can be used for two or three days after preparation, if kept carefully excluded from the light, in a portfolio or drawer.

PLAIN SILVER SOLUTION.

This can be used with the prepared chloride of sodium paper, sold by dealers in Photographic materials, and consists of dissolving $2\frac{1}{2}$ ounces of nitrate of silver in twelve ounces of water. This is also used for silvering the albumen paper, which is prepared as described on page 61.

The chloride of sodium paper and the albumen paper is silvered by laying each sheet separately on the silver solution, contained in a flat dish, and allowing it to float for five minutes, care being observed that no air-bubbles collect under the paper.

The silver solutions must always be filtered through cotton before applying them to the paper. It is only necessary to filter such quantity as may be wanted for immediate use.

The bottles containing the silver solutions should be blackened over with black asphaltum varnish, to exclude the light, and always kept as much as possible in a dark place. Papers may be silvered in a light room, though not where the direct rays of the sun can fall on them.

TO PREPARE THE ALBUMEN PAPER.

Take the whites of three or four fresh eggs, and beat them with a glass rod or flat piece of glass until the article becomes of a frothy consistency. Remove the froth, and place it in a cool place, and allow it to return to its liquid state again, in a long bottle.

Pour off the clear portion of this, and add to

every fluid ounce say from one to four ounces of water, according to the strength of albumen that is required. To each ounce of this fluid of albumen and water, which will readily combine, add fifteen grains of hydrochlorate of ammonia: filter. For salting paper with albumen, it should be floated three or four minutes. Thin paper is generally preferred for the purpose.

SILVERING ALBUMEN PAPER.

Albumen paper must always be silvered with plain silver, of the proportions given on page 59. It must also be floated on the surface of the solution for four or five minutes, never brushed in, as in the ammonia nitrate process.

After using this silver solution with the albumen paper, there will a milky appearance be observed, which can readily be removed by mixing a small quantity of kaolin or china-clay with the silver, and, before using it, filter it clear.

If the proper manipulation is attended to in the use of the albumenized paper, the results will be far more pleasing than by the ammonia nitrate process. The trouble and time required, however, is much greater in the former than in the latter. Therefore the ammonia nitrate is generally adopted by the profession as more certain in its results.

PRINTING FROM NEGATIVES.

The usual time required to print a picture from a good negative, under the most favorable circumstances, is about four minutes. It is proper to state, however, what are the most favorable circumstances. They are good paper, good silvering solution, and a clear sun-light, with all the necessary details of the practice carefully followed, as in the foregoing directions.

Negatives may be printed with a subdued light, and printed well, as there are many cloudy days when the prints are wanted. Of course, the time of exposure must be prolonged, and even an hour may sometimes be required to produce the necessary depth of color on the paper.

The color which is to be obtained on the print before it is ready to remove from the printing frame, is of considerable importance. The best prints are generally those which are left long enough to assume a depth of shade nearly the intensity that may be wanted when finished and dried, rather darker than the color desired, in order that the time occupied in the toning bath shall fix the color, to lighten the shades only in a slight degree.

Prints that are too dark on removal from the printing frame, can be rendered sufficiently light by a long action of the toning bath. But such prints will be the more likely to assume a yellow hue, and ultimately fade. The shortest time in the toning bath to produce the desired shade and color is recommended. Therefore prints should not generally be overdone or over-printed when one toning bath is used.

The kind of printing frames recommended are described on page 109.

After the picture is removed from the printing frame, it must be carefully excluded from the light, by placing it in a portfolio or drawer, or where no vapors can reach it. A number of prints may be prepared and laid aside, and all toned or fixed at once.

TONING OR FIXING THE PRINT.

The beautiful tone or color of the prints in their removal from the printing frame, has been a subject of remark by many operators, and various efforts have been made to preserve that most to be desired color, yet it has never been accomplished.

As soon as the fixing solution comes in contact with the paper, a great change takes place, which does indeed arrest the progress of the light, but produces another and entirely diverse change. As the art progresses, some devotee may luckily arrive at the discovery of fixing the exact tone and color seen on its removal from the printing frame.

The first operation of toning the picture is to place it in a bath of clear water, in a dark room, of course, or in a salt solution of two or three ounces of salt to one quart of water. This removes all the chloride of silver not acted upon by the light. They should remain in the salted solution only a short time, say one or two minutes, then place them in a bath of pure water to remove the superfluous salt. This plan of first placing the print in a solution of common salt may be omitted. It may be placed immediately on removal from the frame into the toning bath, or it may be laid in a portfolio, and excluded entirely from the light for several hours, then placed in the toning bath. After which they may be brought out in the light and placed in the toning bath, as found on page 94, and allowed to remain there until the desired color is attained, which will vary according to the strength of the bath and the depth of the print—

generally from ten to thirty minutes for ordinary prints, yet sometimes one or two hours are necessary. They must be carefully watched in the bath, and as soon as sufficient time has elapsed to produce the desired tone, remove them to a bath of clear water.

WASHING POSITIVE PRINTS.

This portion of the photographic process is of great importance, for unless the prints are well washed, so as to remove every trace of hyposulphite of soda, they will invariably fade or turn yellow. Various methods are adopted to remove the hyposulphite, but the plan most likely to insure that result is of course recommended. The longer the prints remain in the water, and the oftener they are changed, will of course more effectually remove the destroying agent. Strange, indeed, that the very substance, hyposulphite of soda, which adds so much beauty to the Photograph, should be the very one to cause its destruction.

The most expeditious method is to place the print on a piece of plate-glass, and allow a stream of water to fall upon it for a few minutes. Then press it between clean white blotting-paper, repeating the operation two or three times. It has been found that the oftener the water is changed in the washing process, the more beautiful the tones of the prints. Nor should they remain for any great length of time in one vessel of water. The better plan to adopt, when it is possible, is to place the prints in a flat dish or tub, where they will float, and where a constant stream of water is running in, and of course another stream discharging as fast as the supply is given. A very small stream will suffice. By the foregoing arrangements, all those spots and stains so frequently met with will be avoided.

The washing of Photographs may sometimes be completed by placing them in a large vessel of water, and allowing them to remain for several hours. This can only be done after they have been first immersed in several changes of water, say five or ten minutes in each. Still another plan of removing the hyposulphite of soda is highly recommended in the immersion of the prints in warm water. By changing it often with cold water, and allowing it to remain for about an hour in warm water, it will most effectually remove the traces of the soda. Lastly, press each print between two thick pieces of plate-glass, and hang them up to dry.

All these various methods are adopted by the profession, and the successful operator will follow those most convenient of practice, carefully observing, in order to produce excellent results, that the prints shall not remain more than ten minutes in the first or second bath of pure water, because the chemicals which pass into the water, and are so necessary to remove in order to fix the impression permanently, are likely to injure the beauty and tone of the picture.

DRYING, VARNISHING, AND MOUNTING THE PICTURE.

The prints may be hung up in the clothes-pins to dry, but not in the sun. As soon as they are well dried, place them in a portfolio, or between leaves of white paper, and press them under some object, so that they shall not wrinkle. They are then ready for mounting and varnishing.

The varnish for pictures is made as described on page 100, and may be laid on the picture before it is cut in the shape required, or it may be effected after it is on the card-board.

A solution of dextrine, prepared as described on page 104, is the best for holding the print in its place; yet simple gum-arabic will answer if it has been thoroughly strained and cleared of all particles of dust.

The shape of the print may be made by laying a mat or border over it of any desired size, then marking with a pencil, and afterwards cutting it carefully with the scissors. Or it may be laid on a piece of plate-glass, with the mat laid over it, and cutting it into shape with a sharp penknife.

In pasting the print upon the card-board, great care must be observed that no wrinkles are allowed on the surface, as they will invariably injure the print. After the prints are pasted on the boards, they should be laid under a pressure, so that great smoothness of surface shall be attained. A warm flat-iron is sometimes used with good success, by laying a piece of white paper over each print, and carefully pressing it smooth.

CHAPTER IV.

TO COPY DAGUERREOTYPES AND OTHER PICTURES INTO PHOTOGRAPHS—ON ENLARGING PICTURES—TO ENLARGE PICTURES FROM DAGUERREOTYPES, AMBROTYPES, OR PHOTOGRAPHS—AND TO PRODUCE PHOTOGRAPHS FROM THEM—TO MAKE LIFE-SIZE PHOTOGRAPHS ON PAPER—IRON PHOTOGRAPHS, OR INSTANTANEOUS PRINTING—ON TAKING STEREOSCOPE PICTURES, PHOTOGRAPHIC VIEWS, ETC., ETC.

The copying of Daguerreotypes into other Daguerreotypes, has long been in practice. Latterly they have been successfully copied into Ambrotypes and Photographs. But Photography has gone still further, and life-size pictures are now produced which, when painted by the skilful artist, have rivalled the creations of most painters, both in the correctness and faithfulness of the likeness, which must needs be infallible.

The last great achievement of the Photographic Art, is the production of life-size, full-length portraits. This is accomplished by the means of the new solar camera, lately introduced, which bids fair to supersede all other methods of enlarging pictures. Those who may not possess the new solar camera, can adopt the following process, which will be found very useful and practical.

TO ENLARGE PICTURES FROM DAGUERREOTYPES, AMBROTYPES, OR PHOTOGRAPHS—AND TO PRODUCE PHOTOGRAPHS FROM THEM.

The following apparatus will be required for the process, viz.:

One quarter-plate tube, and lens.
One whole-plate camera box.
One or two mirrors to be used as reflectors.
One camera box, capable of holding a glass 14 by 17 inches.

The pictures or portraits more frequently required to be enlarged are the ordinary Daguerreotypes, from the fact that these are the kind of portraiture the longest in use. Many are desirous of obtaining portraits of their deceased friends, life-size, and the demand for that class of pictures is consequently greater than any other.

The plan more easily adopted, is first to take a negative from the Daguerreotype of the ordinary half or whole plate size, which is effected by the use of a quarter-plate tube on a whole-size camera box. Place the picture to be enlarged, whether it be a Daguerreotype, Ambrotype, or Photograph, in the direct rays of the sun, or by reflecting the sun upon it with a mirror, then bringing the camera box as near the picture as will be required to produce the desired size; the focus being taken, a negative can easily be obtained by exposure of thirty seconds to a minute and a half. The negative should be as large as possible if on a half-plate, in order that it may be enlarged to life size by the next operation.

From the print now obtained, which must be first pasted on a card-board, another negative can be produced, either of the cabinet or life size, with the quarter tube attached to the camera box, which must be capable of holding glasses of 11 by 14 inches, and 14 by 17. Place the pictures in the direct rays of the sun, or use a reflector as before, and any size may be taken, up to the size of life,—showing, of course, only the head and shoulders.

The print from this negative will not be so distinct in the outline as though it was taken from life; yet it will retain all the outline and sufficient of the details for all purposes of painting, and it may be printed either upon paper or canvas with the same facility as ordinary Photographic printing.

In order to insure a more perfect negative, it may sometimes become necessary to use more than one mirror as a reflector of the sun's rays upon the surface of the picture. The more powerful the reflection the more distinct will be the negative. The re-developing with bi-chloride of mercury, as given on page 92, is highly recommended in this process.

A negative may be taken without the direct rays of the sun from any picture; but, in enlarging, the powerful light of the sun is deemed almost indispensable, as it greatly facilitates the process, and renders the time required much shorter, and secures a more intense and definite negative.

Should the Daguerreotype be an imperfect one, as is frequently the case, of course all the imperfections will be magnified, yet they can be entirely removed by the skill of the painter.

The usual time required for taking the negative, life-size, will vary from a minute to ten minutes. In consequence of the large size and the long distance of the ground glass from the lenses, the time of exposure in the camera is greatly augmented.

IRON PHOTOGRAPHS, OR INSTANTANEOUS PRINTING OF NEGATIVES WITH A DEVELOPER.

A process has lately been introduced for printing negatives, with the use of a preparation of iron: hence the name Iron Photographs. This process, however, is a revival of an old one. It will be found very useful on many occasions, when expedition is required, as a negative may be taken and the positive picture printed, washed, toned, and dried in the same time as an ordinary Ambrotype. The process is as follows:

Water	1 pint.
Citric acid	1 ounce.
Ammonia citrate of iron	$\frac{1}{2}$ ounce.
Concentrated ammonia	1 ounce.

Mix these ingredients, and filter, and keep in a glass-stoppered bottle, excluded from the light of day.

Apply this solution with a flat camel's-hair brush on one side only of the photographic paper, carefully laying it on even by brushing it in both directions. Then hang it up to dry in a dark room. When dry, it may be cut into suitable sizes for printing, and kept in a portfolio. The paper will assume a yellow color. Print with the ordinary printing frames, but only for a short time, until the faint outlines appear. Remove from the printing frame, and apply the developing solution either by immersing in a flat dish, or pouring it on the paper after laying it upon glass.

THE DEVELOPING SOLUTION.

Nitrate of silver	$\frac{1}{2}$ ounce.
Water	1 pint.
Aqua ammonia	$\frac{1}{4}$ ounce.

Filter the solution, and use over again.

THE TONING BATH.

Hyposulphite of soda	1 ounce.
Water	1 pint.
Nitro-muriatic acid	10 drops.

Wash the print well after developing, and place it in this toning bath for a short time, and the color will be changed from the deep reddish hue that it has assumed by the developer, to a purple color.

The print must now be washed quickly in three or four waters, and placed between sheets of blotting-paper, and dried by the spirit-lamp. Should the tone not be desirable, a modification of the toning bath may be made by changing the proportions of hyposulphite and the addition of chloride of gold. The tone may be improved sometimes by exposure of the print for a few seconds to the direct rays of the sun. The addition of a saturated solution of gallic acid to the developer, in small quantities, will change the tone; but it cannot be used over again. Therefore only mix enough for each print as it may be required for use.

The sepia tone may be given these prints by omitting the hyposulphite bath entirely, merely washing them in water thoroughly after developing, but they will be more liable to fade.

Photographs by this new process may be printed from a weak negative, and even an ambrotype impression will answer. The tone of the prints will not be equal to those printed by the old process; but sometimes expedition may be required, and Photographs can be taken and finished as soon as Daguerreotypes or Ambrotypes.

THE STEREOSCOPE.

Stereoscope pictures are considered by some operators as the most valued of the productions of the Photographic Art. If they are properly executed, they are indeed the most curious and instructive of any branch of Photography, though they have not received that attention in this country which they have merited,—mainly, however, from the fact that few operators have devoted much attention to their production. The most pleasing are Photograph views.

The stereoscope is an instrument invented by Prof. Wheatstone, for combining two slightly dissimilar images, so that out of two flat pictures *one* apparently real or solid object is produced—having all the projections, concavatures, and other peculiarities of the object itself, and standing out in all the strength and solidity of an actual tangible object.

The reason why two flat images should produce the effect of solidity, and a slight consideration of the best means of producing these flat pictures, so that they shall produce in the most proper manner this extraordinary result, will now be given.

Ordinary vision may be considered under the two heads of Monocular, or vision by one eye, and Binocular, or vision by two eyes. If we look through a telescope, microscope, or single opera-glass, or close one eye, we have monocular vision; and by using two eyes, or spectacles, or double opera-glasses, we have binocular vision.

Let us first consider monocular vision. If we close one eye and look at objects, we perceive them by their forms, sizes, colors, and gradations of light and shade; and reason and experience tell us that these appearances vary as the objects are near or distant from us. We find that as objects recede they become smaller, apparently, in size, and this decrease in size is according to fixed laws, upon which perspective is based. We also observe that light and shade are less marked, the colors less brilliant, the details less clear, and the whole of the objects less distinct; and according to these changes do we estimate relative distances. Upon this principle the artist, in his landscape, paints his distant objects small, vague, and indistinct, while the foreground is brought out strongly with abundance of detail; and in proportion as this is done skilfully, we admire it as an imitation of nature. There is, also, another means of judging of distance. The eye, like other optical instruments, has constantly to change its focus, according to distances to which it is directed, and this change of focus is another means of estimating distance.

Stereoscopic pictures may be taken either with one or two cameras. If the object be still-life, a statue, or edifice, then one camera will do better than two, for you may set the camera at any point and work away until you produce a satisfactory impression. Having obtained that, move the camera to the other point of view, and again work until you have achieved your object. But if you should have a picture of living objects to take, it is very desirable to produce the *two* pictures simultaneously by two cameras; for taking a view of a street, for instance, where figures are accidentally introduced, you might have them in one picture and not in the other, or misplaced, unless you obtained both pictures at the same time. But for portraits, though it is desirable to take both impressions at once, it is not necessary. And now comes the important inquiry, how far removed should the cameras be from each other in order to produce the best effect? or, in other words, how wide should the stereoscopic angle be? This is a question often put, but not so easily answered. Strictly speaking, the natural standard may easily be cited, and an answer based on it be given. The eyes are $2\frac{1}{2}$ inches apart, and as each camera is to represent an eye, the centres of the two lenses should never be more than that separated. This is the strict theoretical doctrine laid down by Sir D. Brewster, nevertheless it is very seldom adopted in practice. It has been stated, that the more dissimilar the two stereoscopic images are, the greater the relief. Now, dissimilarity of image is obtained by widening the distance between the two cameras, and the greater the width or angle the greater the relief. As the stereoscope is chiefly valued for the production of this relief, the generality of stereoscopic pictures have been and are taken at too wide an angle, so that *monstrous* instead of natural relief is the result. If two pictures are taken at the same angle, no relief is obtained but that which is due to the magnifying power of the lenses. Increase the angle a little, and still greater relief is produced; increase the angle still more, and so on until you have passed the angle that produces natural relief, and reached that which produces monstrosity.

Nearly all stereoscopes will have more or less of imperfection in the detail, owing to the fact that no two pair of eyes view the same pictures in the same focus. Hence we find some persons who cannot see the stereoscope pictures at all.

PHOTOGRAPH VIEWS.

Views by the Photographic process are attracting the attention of the artists in this country, and deservedly so. They are easily taken, because an ample supply of light is always obtained. The only objection is the necessity of transporting the various solutions to the localities where the view is to be taken. This difficulty is overcome by the new dry processes which have been published lately. The albumen process on paper, page 61, is highly recommended for views, as the tone of those pictures is more appropriate for this style of Photographs.

It is not necessary here to enter into the details of the processes. Suffice it to say, that the same collodions are to be used, and the same developers, as in the process for taking portraits. The lenses of the ordinary camera, however, must be changed to convert it into a view camera. It is done simply by removing entirely the set of lenses in the rear of the tube, and placing the front lens in their stead, and reversing them. It will also be necessary to put a diaphragm, with a very small opening, in front of the tube, or near the location of the front lens. The time of exposure required in the camera with a small diaphragm, will necessarily be somewhat extended in order to produce vigorous negatives. The use of the diaphragm is absolutely necessary in order to correct the perspective of near and distant objects. Also to cut off a portion of the diffused light, which would otherwise injure the negative.

CHAPTER V.

ON THE PREPARATION OF NEGATIVE COLLODIONS—THE FORMULÆ FOR NEGATIVE COLLODIONS—MIXING VARIOUS COLLODIONS—DISSOLVING THE IODIDES—DOUBLE IODIDE COLLODIONS—THE CELEBRATED GERMAN PROCESS COMPLETE—THE NEGATIVE DEVELOPING SOLUTIONS — RE-DEVELOPING PROCESS — BICHLORIDE OF MERCURY AS A RE-DEVELOPER—FIXING SOLUTION—THE TONING BATHS—THE AMMONIA NITRATE OF SILVER SOLUTION.

This chapter will be devoted to careful and detailed formulæ for the preparation of the negative collodions, the developing solutions, and including all the various receipts necessary to be well understood in the practice of the Photographic Art.

Indeed, this chapter will assume one most entirely of reference, and, as will be seen, it must frequently require mention in other portions of this work.

NEGATIVE COLLODIONS.

For the preparation of negative collodions, we shall only give the proportions. The manner of dissolving the sensitive chemicals will generally be left to the judgment and experience of the operator.

THE AMMONIA COLLODION.

No. 1. Plain collodion . . . 1 ounce.
Iodide of ammonia . . . 6 grains.
Bromide of ammonia . . 3 grains.

With the nitrate of silver bath neutral, and of a strength of 50 grains of silver to each ounce of water.

CADMIUM COLLODION.

No. 2. Plain collodion . . . 1 ounce.
Iodide of cadmium . . 7 grains.
Bromide of cadmium . . 3 grains.

Nitrate bath 50 grains to the ounce.

This collodion is greatly in use in warm climates.

No. 3. Plain collodion . . . 1 ounce.
Iodide of potassium . . 8 grains.
Bromide of ammonia . . 3 grains.

Bath of 40 grains to the ounce.

This collodion is highly recommended for negatives when combined equally with the ammonia collodion No. 1. It will be found to work in some baths when no other collodion will succeed. It may be used also for Ambrotypes.

The practice of the most successful operators has taught them that the mixing of two collodions of diverse proportions, and made of different chemicals, will be found the most useful, and work with more certainty. The author himself would, therefore, enjoin this hint upon those who may practice from the foregoing formulæ.

THE COMPOUND CADMIUM COLLODION.

No. 4. Plain collodion . . . 1 ounce.
Iodide of cadmium . . 6 grains.
Bromide of cadmium . . 3 grains.
Iodide of potassium . . 5 grains.
Tincture of iodine . . . 5 drops.

Nitrate bath of 50 grains to the ounce. The bath to be iodized with iodide of cadmium.

Dissolve the iodide of potassium in water, and the cadmium in alcohol.

The foregoing collodion is the one highly recommended for use, especially in warm latitudes. It is the most durable, and it improves by age, retaining its working qualities for several months. The author has adopted the cadmium collodion, in many instances with great success, especially when it is combined in equal parts with the ammonia collodion No. 1.

To unite the sensitive ingredients with all collodions, it is recommended to dissolve them first in a small quantity of alcohol when they are soluble in that substance, and only use water when they will not otherwise dissolve. Always dissolve the bromides first, and add the iodides to the same solution. The iodide of ammonia and bromide of ammonia will dissolve in alcohol if a small quantity of water is added. Iodide and bromide of cadmium will dissolve readily in alcohol alone.

A DOUBLE-IODIZED COLLODION.

The following formula is compounded in a different manner from any other, and is one that is highly recommended. Prepare two bottles of collodion separately, as follows:

No. 1. Plain collodion . . 1 ounce.
        Bromide of potassium . 5 grains. } Dissolved
        Iodide of potassium. . 8 grains. } in water.

No. 2. Plain collodion .
        Iodide of ammonia . 5 grains. } Dissolved
        Iodide of cadmium . 3 grains. } in water.

No. 1 will produce clear negatives, and perhaps rather weak. No. 2 will produce one very intense.

But mix these two collodions in equal proportions after they have well settled, and the most perfect half-tints are obtained. Should it be desirable to produce a negative of more intensity, use a larger proportion of No. 2. In like manner, if a mixture of equal proportions produces too much intensity, then increase the quantity of No. 1.

It will be found on using the two collodions above, separately, that as one will produce a weak negative, and the other a deep one, they can be so modified by uniting them in the proper proportions, that any degree of intensity may be obtained.

THE GERMAN PROCESS.

The following method of preparing negative collodion has been found to be very excellent in its results, and is known as the German process, so modified and rendered practical that any operator can work it successfully.

The plain collodion is to be made with 10 ounces of ether and 5 of alcohol, rendered of the requisite consistency by the addition of gun-cotton.

TO SENSITIZE THE COLLODION.

Nitrate of silver dissolved in water . 50 grains.
Iodide of ammonia dissolved in water 40 grains.

Mix the two solutions, and wash the precipitate

in several waters; lastly, wash in alcohol. Then make the following compound:

Alcohol at 95°	2 fluid ounces.
Iodide of ammonia	100 grains.
Bromide of ammonia	40 grains.

When dissolved, add the iodide of silver, and agitate the whole for several minutes; then filter through common filtering-paper, and add the liquid to 20 ounces plain collodion; agitate the collodion for a short time, and add to it as follows:

Fluoride of ammonia	40 drops.
Tincture of iodine	10 drops.

This iodized collodion may be used in 12 hours, but is much improved by standing 3 or 4 days. The tincture of iodine used in the collodion is simply a saturated solution of alcohol at 95°, with pure crystals of iodine.

NITRATE BATH.

Distilled water	56 fluid oz.
Nitrate of silver	$4\frac{1}{2}$ oz. by weight.
Dissolve the silver in 8 oz. of the	56 oz. of water.
Then add iodide of ammonia	10 grains.
White sugar or rock-candy	120 grains.

When dissolved, add the remainder of the water, and in this condition let the bath stand 12 hours;

then filter through common filtering-paper, add 30 drops glacial acetic acid, and it is fit for use.

DEVELOPING SOLUTION FOR NEGATIVES.

Pure soft water	16 ounces.
Sulphate of iron	1 ounce.
Alcohol at 95°	1 ounce.
Acetic acid, No. 8	2 ounces.

First dissolve the iron, then add the remaining properties, and when filtered it is ready for use.

FIXING SOLUTION.

This is simply any quantity of water saturated with hyposulphite of soda.

RE-DEVELOPING.

The negative is re-developed after it has been cleared up. Make a saturated solution of gallic acid in distilled water 1 ounce, then add 30 drops of the following solution:

Distilled water	1 ounce.
Nitrate of silver	35 grains.

When this solution is filtered, it may be used as follows:—After the negative has been fixed and washed, pour on it of the re-developing solution a quantity sufficient to cover the plate, and keep it on until the required intensity is obtained, then wash with water and dry. In developing and re-developing, the solutions must be kept gently and constantly moving on the plate; for if allowed to stand still, or to remain for any length of time on one portion of the plate more than on other parts, the plate is liable to lines or streaks.

This re-developing process is not recommended, and if the collodion and bath are properly made, need never be adopted except it may be in dark weather, or when a child's likeness is taken. For it will always be found that the resulting negative is never so well adapted for printing. Therefore, as soon as one finds that he cannot procure negatives sufficiently intense in an ordinary exposure without re-developing, he may be assured there is some portion of his chemicals at fault. The first opportunity should be embraced to remedy the difficulty: first, by changing the nature of the nitrate bath, then the collodion and developing agent.

THE NEGATIVE DEVELOPING SOLUTIONS.

The developing solutions which are required for the negative pictures are not very numerous. The one mostly in use is composed of protosulphite of

NEGATIVE DEVELOPING SOLUTIONS. 89

iron and acetic acid. With this alone, and the various modifications, all the different varieties of negatives are produced in this country. In Europe the developing solutions mostly in use are composed of pyrogallic acid.

The developing process must be thoroughly understood before good results can be obtained. And, first, the nature of the collodion and the nitrate bath must be known in order to form the developer so as to produce the best results with that combination. The following formula will be the best adapted for working the neutral bath of 50 grains to the ounce, with the ammonia or cadmium collodion, as prepared on page 82.

Protosulphite of iron	2 ounces.
Water	1 quart.
Acetic acid, No. 8	6 ounces.

The iron is first dissolved in the water and filtered, and the acetic acid is added in the above proportions, but only as it may be required for use. It will not develop properly if mixed and allowed to remain for several hours. It may sometimes require a small quantity of alcohol to cause the solution to flow evenly over the plate. But the addition of the alcohol lessens the intensity of the picture, therefore it is best to avoid its introduction as much as possible. Indeed, its use has been abandoned by good operators.

By increasing the quantity of iron, the developing process proceeds more rapidly, and by lessening the quantity of acetic acid it is modified.

In order, therefore, to ascertain the requisite quantity of each ingredient that may be necessary for the particular combinations of collodions and baths, it will be proper to vary the proportions of iron and acetic acid. By a few changes in the proportions, and a few trials, nearly all varieties of collodion may be made to produce a good negative, if the bath is of the requisite strength and all other due proportions are observed.

There will, however, be found another formula for re-developing negatives on page 91, which is given in addition to the foregoing mainly with a view to enable any person to obtain an intense negative, even if their chemicals are not properly combined.

RE-DEVELOPING PROCESS.

Frequently the negatives, after being developed by the foregoing solutions, will not assume that degree of intensity that is desired. They may still be made more intense by continuing the process of developing in the following manner:

Prepare two solutions as follows, viz.:

No. 1. Water . . . . . . 8 ounces.
Protosulphite of iron . . 2 ounces.

Dissolve the iron and filter.

The second solution is as follows:

No. 2. Nitrate of silver . . . ¼ ounce.
Water . . . . . . 8 ounces.

The re-developing is attended with some difficulty, as there is great danger in producing lines or streaks on the negative.

The following cautions must be observed:—After the first process of developing, wash carefully with a large quantity of water, still keeping the plate in the dark room upon the levelling-stand, or in the hand, and pour over its surface enough of the solution No. 1 to nearly cover it; then quickly pour enough of No. 2 to mix with it upon the plate, which must have a little motion in order to flow over the whole plate as quickly as possible. It will be seen that no perceptible action takes place on the application of the iron solution; but as soon as the silver is added, a quick and energetic action commences, and the intensity is increased to any desired depth. Great care must be observed not to continue this process too far, as the negative will become too intense, and full of lines and streaks. As soon as sufficient intensity is produced, wash quickly with water all traces of the developer.

BICHLORIDE OF MERCURY AS A RE-DEVELOPER.

Make a saturated solution of bichloride of mercury, and always have it in readiness in a glass-stoppered bottle.

This can be used with great success in copying Daguerreotypes or Ambrotypes into negatives. The solution must be reduced considerably from the full strength of the saturated solution, but only the quantity required for use. The exact amount of dilution will depend upon the strength of the negative after it is developed by the protosulphite of iron developer. The plate is first developed in the usual manner as soon as it is removed from the camera, then carefully washed, and, before the light has fallen upon it, a weak solution of the bichloride of mercury is poured quickly over it. It will assume a deeper intensity immediately; and when sufficiently so, it is to be washed and fixed in the hyposulphite in the usual manner. All negatives, rendered intense by the application of bichloride of mercury, will assume a deep bluish-black color, which can be modified by changing the strength of this re-developing agent.

FIXING SOLUTION.

This is always a saturated solution of hyposulphite of soda.

The plate is to be thoroughly washed with water after developing, and laid carefully in a flat dish containing the hyposulphite of soda; and as soon as the iodide of silver is dissolved from the surface, which may be known by its becoming clear from that milky appearance, it must then be immediately washed entirely free from the least traces of soda.

Then dried—or it may be varnished before drying, with a solution of gum-arabic, of the consistency of collodion which has been strained. Of course, the gum-arabic is to be poured over the surface in the same manner as collodion.

TONING BATHS.

The most useful and practical toning bath for paper, prepared with the ammonia nitrate of silver solution, is composed as follows:

Water	1 quart.
Nitrate of silver	60 grains.
Chloride of gold	60 grains.
Or four bottles of the ordinary chloride of gold.	
Hyposulphite of soda . . .	2 ounces.

In preparing the foregoing bath, the following method should be adopted to insure the most complete success.

Dissolve the hyposulphite of soda in about four or six ounces of the water taken from the quart, and the chloride of gold in about four ounces of water, in separate bottles. Convert the 60 grains of nitrate of silver into the chloride of silver, by dissolving it first in three or four ounces of water, to which add 60 grains of common salt. Wash the precipitate in water three or four times, then pour off all the water, leaving the white precipitate, which is the pure chloride of silver. Now pour this solution of chloride of silver and hyposulphite into the remaining portion of the water, and add the chloride of gold in solution to it. It will assume at first a wine color, and may appear of a darker hue in a few moments. It is now ready to receive the printed picture from the printing frame, or it may be first immersed in salt and water, as described on page 64.

This toning bath is intended only for paper salted

in the manner described on page 57, and silvered with the ammonia nitrate of silver solution, as described below. When not in use, it should be kept from the light in a glass-stoppered bottle. This bath, when once prepared in the foregoing manner, will improve by age and use, for the immersion of every print tends to increase the quantity of chloride of silver. A bottle of chloride of gold must be added occasionally, dissolved in six or eight ounces of water.

PREPARATION OF THE AMMONIA NITRATE OF SILVER SOLUTION.

Nitrate of silver . . . . . 2 ounces.
Distilled water . . . . . 1 pint.

Dissolve the silver in the pint of water, and pour out about two ounces into a separate bottle for future use.

Now add of strong concentrated aqua ammonia, a few drops at a time, to the fourteen ounces solution of silver and water. A dark brown precipitate is formed at first, which must be stirred with a glass rod, or, if in a bottle, it may be shaken. Continue to add more of the aqua ammonia, and stir the solution until it remains perfectly clear. Then add the two ounces which were reserved for use, as referred to above. This will cause the solution to be slightly turbid, which can be filtered perfectly clear, and it is then ready for use. This preparation must be kept entirely excluded from the light of day.

This solution must be filtered, and only in sufficient quantity for immediate use.

A more sensitive preparation may be made by adding to the above about six drops of nitric acid.

CHAPTER VI.

DETAILS OF THE VARIOUS RECIPES IN THE PHOTOGRAPHIC PROCESS—QUICK METHOD OF SILVERING AND PRINTING PAPER—BEST METHOD OF SALTING PAPER—TEST FOR GOOD COLLODION OR GUN-COTTON—VARNISH FOR POSITIVES ON PAPER—INSTANTANEOUS PRINTING PROCESS—NEW METHOD OF VARNISHING POSITIVES — TO RESTORE PRINTS THAT HAVE CHANGED COLOR—CLEANING GLASS PLATES—TO VARNISH NEGATIVES—DEXTRINE PASTE FOR MOUNTING PHOTOGRAPHS—GUM-ARABIC AND GELATINE—TO RESTORE SILVER FROM OLD SOLUTIONS—TO REMOVE WATER FROM COLLODION, AND TO PURIFY IT—TEST OF HYPOSULPHITE OF SILVER IN POSITIVE PRINTS—PRINTING VARIOUS BACKGROUNDS.

This chapter will be devoted to the variety of practice in the Photographic Art. Many recipes will be given of the various forms of operating. Many will be found useful, and it is trusted that none will omit to note down the variety here because they number so many. These must necessarily be given promiscuously, from the fact that no process here written has any peculiar relation to another.

AN EXPEDITIOUS METHOD OF SILVERING PAPER AND PRINTING THE SAME.

Employ the ammonia nitrate of silver, the usual strength, and fasten the paper already salted upon a flat piece of board, by means of a pin or small nail, at each corner. Then, with a ball of clean cotton dipped in a solution of silver just filtered, and placed in an open flat dish, carefully rub the paper in all directions. Then dry it quickly by a fire in the usual daylight. As soon as it is dry, place it immediately in the printing frame, and expose to the sun's rays. This will insure a picture with very little delay; and if proper care has been observed in the operation, very excellent results may be obtained. Many successful artists have adopted the foregoing process with marked success.

THE BEST METHOD OF SALTING PHOTOGRAPHIC PAPER.

Always use the hydrochlorate of ammonia (sal ammoniac) in salting paper, and never over 90 grains to the quart of water. A larger quantity impairs the tone.

This preparation of sodium has been found to produce the best results, from the fact that it is in a purer state than any other known forms of salt. Hence it should take the preference of all others in the salting process.

The addition of gelatine to the salting solution is strongly recommended, say about one grain to every ounce of water. The gelatine should be of the purest quality, and it should first be dissolved in warm water, and added to the salting solution, which itself must be warmed if in the winter season.

Always filter the salting solution, so as to avoid any spots of dust or foreign substances that may collect in the dish.

TEST FOR GOOD COLLODION OR GUN-COTTON.

There is a sure test, and one that it is well to remember and apply, in making collodion. After the gun-cotton is well dissolved in the ether and alcohol, and of the requisite thickness, pour a small quantity of the plain collodion on a piece of glass, allowing it to drain off in the same manner as in coating the plate with sensitized collodion.

If the glass appears perfectly clear and transparent after it is dried and held up to transmitted light, it may be used for working collodion; but if there should appear any milkiness or opacity on the surface of the glass, there is a fault of the gun-cotton or the alcohol or ether. Unless a perfect, clear, and transparent film is obtained, the collodion, when properly sensitized, will not furnish good results. The addition of a small quantity of alcohol will sometimes remedy the defect.

VARNISH FOR POSITIVE PHOTOGRAPHS ON PAPER.

The best varnish for paper pictures is undoubtedly gum-arabic and gelatine.

The gum-arabic must be allowed to dissolve thoroughly, then with warm water dissolve the gelatine, using only a small quantity. The proportions are as follows:

Gum-arabic dissolved, and about the consistency of collodion	1 ounce.
Gelatine	2 drachms.

Dissolve and filter through a cloth every time before using. To be laid on with a flat brush made of hogs' bristles.

INSTANTANEOUS PRINTING PROCESS.

In dark, cloudy weather, or in winter, it is sometimes desirable to print positives, and the following method will be found to be useful, as pictures can be produced in the least portion of daylight. It is as follows:—Float the papers each for five minutes in a solution of bichloride of mercury, prepared as follows:

Saturated solution of bichloride of mercury 6 drachms.
Water . . . . 1 pint.

Silver it in a plain silver solution, 40 grains to the ounce of water. But it must be so done in a dark room, and the lamp carefully screened by means of a yellow glass. Expose only for about two to ten seconds in summer, and not more than a minute in winter, and then in a very subdued light. Of course the paper must be placed in the printing frame in a darkened room, and the frame itself carefully excluded from the light during the operation, except the time required to make the impression. Remove the picture still in the dark room, when it will appear very feeble, but it is seen to be developed by means of a solution of sulphate of iron, as follows:

Sulphate of iron	½ ounce.
Water	1 pint.
Glacial acetic acid	¼ ounce.

Develop until the picture is of the required depth of color, then wash, and immediately fix with hyposulphite of soda; and finally, carefully wash, as in the ordinary process.

NEW METHOD OF VARNISHING POSITIVE PHOTOGRAPHS ON PAPER.

Dissolve by a slow heat two ounces of white wax and add two ounces of common Venice turpentine, and stir the mixture well. This, when cool, will be of the consistency of paste. After the Photographs are dried, spread this paste evenly over the surface with a brush, and rub it with a piece of woollen flannel; hang it up to dry in a warm room for six or twelve hours. The smell of the turpentine soon leaves the print, and when dry it may be rubbed hard with dry flannel until a fine polish is obtained. This process of varnishing Photographs not only greatly improves them, but also preserves them from liability to fade.

TO RESTORE PRINTS THAT HAVE CHANGED COLOR.

Wash the print well, and immerse it in a solution prepared as follows:

Water . . . . 1 quart.
Saturated solution of the bichloride of mercury in muriatic acid . . . } 20 drops.

Remove the picture as soon as the desired purple tone is attained, then carefully wash it in several waters, and dry. Prints that are greatly faded may be restored by this process equal to new.

CLEANING GLASS PLATES.

Some operators experience much difficulty in cleaning the glass plates for negatives. It is a matter which to some is no difficulty, and therefore not much attention is paid to it by those who work successfully. In order to feel perfectly sure that the plates are cleaned, they may be first immersed in a solution composed as follows:

Water . . . . . 1 pint.
Cyanide of potassium . ¼ ounce or 120 grains.
Carbonate of potassium . 240 grains.

By placing all new glasses in this solution for a few minutes all traces of grease or fatty substances are removed. They can then be washed, dried, and cleaned with alcohol in the usual manner. Glasses that have been used may be more readily cleaned by first laying them in water in order to remove the collodion. Then immerse them in the foregoing solution, wash, dry, and clean as usual.

TO VARNISH NEGATIVES.

Negatives may be varnished with the common white negative varnish, or the diamond varnish, sold by all the dealers in photographic materials.

DEXTRINE PASTE FOR MOUNTING PHOTOGRAPHS.

The article known as dextrine is the best in use for pasting Photographs on card-board, from the fact that it is not so liable to cause them to fade. It is made simply by mixing a sufficient quantity of ground dextrine in hot water to render it of the consistency of ordinary paste. Then apply with a brush.

GUM-ARABIC AND GELATINE.

Gum-arabic	8 ounces.
Gelatine	¼ ounce.

Mix and dissolve in hot water, and strain through a cloth before using. This is useful for varnishing the Photograph after it is pasted on the card-board.

By the addition of a little sugar to the above, a paste is formed which may be used for pasting the Photographs on the card-board instead of the dextrine.

TO SEPARATE SILVER FROM OLD COLLODION SILVER BATHS,

FROM THE NITRATE OF SILVER SOLUTION, USED IN PREPARING POSITIVE PAPER, AND FROM THE WATER THAT HAS BEEN USED TO WASH THE PRINTS BEFORE THE IMMERSION IN THE CHLORIDE OF GOLD, ETC.

To the liquid containing the silver add a solution of common salt, until no milkiness is perceptible. This will precipitate the silver in the state of a chloride.

After shaking well, allow this chloride of silver to settle, when the liquid should be poured away, and the precipitate washed several times in clean water. The larger part of the water should now be poured off, and a piece of clean zinc put into the bottle, to which add a few drachms of sulphuric acid. The mixture will immediately effervesce. The zinc is dissolved in a short time, and the chloride of silver will be transformed into metallic silver, in the state of a black powder.

There should be an excess of zinc in the liquid, in order to effect the transformation of all the chloride of silver into metallic silver. This change of the chloride to the metallic state, commences first with that which is in contact with the zinc, which becomes immediately black. It must now stand without shaking, until all the chloride of silver has become uniformly black, when the remaining zinc should be taken out, the liquid poured off, and the silver washed two or three times with water acidulated with sulphuric acid, and finally with clean water.

The silver can be separated from the water by filtering through paper, and is pure. It can be used to prepare nitrate of silver.

TO REMOVE WATER FROM COLLODIONS, AND TO PURIFY OLD COLLODIONS.

A very simple method of removing water which may be found in collodion, is to add a quantity of common saleratus well dried—shake it well and allow it to settle: it will not only remove the water, but greatly improve the quality of the collodion. Many old collodions may be treated in this manner, and greatly benefited.

The quantity of saleratus necessary to add to the collodion is not material—an excess will do no harm; but it is recommended to pour off from the sediment of saleratus into another bottle, to allow it to become clear for use.

The addition of albumen, or the white of an egg,

to a quantity of collodion, and allowed to settle, is also of great benefit to it, especially if it has a tendency to remain thick and turbid.

CHLOROFORM IN COLLODION.

A few drops of chloroform may be added with advantage to collodion when it appears weak on the glass plate, and inclines to break on the application of water in washing off the developer.

TO KNOW IF ALL THE HYPOSULPHITE OF SILVER IS REMOVED FROM THE PRINTS BY WASHING.

When the prints are supposed to be well washed and hung up to dry, allow a few drops of the water from them to fall into a solution of bichloride of mercury. If a white precipitate is formed, the print is not well and sufficiently washed. It will in process of time fade or change color. They should be washed again until no precipitate is seen.

PRINTING BACKGROUNDS OF VARIOUS SHADES.

Any negative with a dark background may be printed with a light one, or *vice versa;* or if an imperfection happens to occur on the background, it may be entirely removed by the printing process, as follows:

First print an impression, and without toning it,

remove it from the printing frame, and cut out the figure of the head and body with a knife or small scissors; in fact, leaving entirely the background separate from the portrait. Fasten this background of paper so cut out around the edges, by means of gum-arabic, upon the negative, and print only the portrait, on another paper of course, leaving the background perfectly white. Now remove this print, and cover the portrait so printed with the piece of paper which was cut out of the first print. This will now become blackened by the action of light, and it must be attached to the second print only at the bottom by gum-arabic. Place it in the printing frame, which contains a clean glass, and expose the background only to the action of light. Of course any degree of shade of background may be attained, and gradations of the light or dark portions can be also given by holding a cloth or piece of card-board over such portion as may be desired of a light color. The card-board should be slightly agitated to prevent any sharp lines on the print.

Figures of various kinds can be represented on the background by means of lace-work, or any open work laid over the background in the second process.

In printing these extra backgrounds, there will necessarily be a sharp outline around the edge of the hair and drapery, which can be removed by retouching with india ink, after the picture is mounted.

PRINTING FRAMES.

There are numerous methods and apparatus in use for holding the negative and paper during the printing process. The common printing board is perhaps the most useful. They can be bought at any of the dealers in photographic materials.

Another kind called pressure frames are rather more expensive, but possess the advantage over the common printing board of giving the operator an opportunity to inspect both ends of his picture during the printing process. Every operator should possess more than one of these printing frames, as the saving of time will amply repay him if he has many prints to make.

Another cheap, convenient, and equally good arrangement for holding the negative and paper, is to take three glasses—say one a full size, being the one having the negative upon it; and then take two glasses, each just half the size of the negative, and have a piece of *very thick heavy* cloth, cut the size of the negative glass, which can be put between it and the two half glasses, and then they can be held together by means of the common spring clothes-pin. The advantage of the two glasses at the back is, that one can be entirely removed while the picture is being examined, and afterwards returned without in the least moving the impression.

CHAPTER VII.

HINTS AND SUGGESTIONS IN REGARD TO THE NEGATIVE PROCESS—IMPERFECTIONS PECULIAR TO NEGATIVES—HOW TO AVOID THEM—CAUTIONS IN TAKING NEGATIVES—HINTS AND SUGGESTIONS IN REGARD TO PRINTING POSITIVES ON PAPER—CAUTIONS IN REGARD TO THEM—IMPERFECTIONS FOUND IN POSITIVES—HOW TO AVOID THEM.

THE art is so full of details in the manipulations, that it is deemed proper to embody in a chapter many hints and suggestions that are very necessary to be well studied by those who adopt the line of practice laid down in this work. In that portion of this Manual devoted to the Ambrotype, will be found a chapter devoted to the failures, &c.; also containing many valuable hints in regard to positives on glass—all of which are valuable as a reference in the negative process.

HINTS AND SUGGESTIONS IN REGARD TO NEGATIVES.

The addition of a small quantity of white sugar, dissolved in water, to the nitrate bath, will sometimes increase the intensity of the negative. The addition of an ounce of alcohol for every quart of water in the bath, will also increase the intensity.

When the collodion will not adhere to the plate on removal from the bath, add a few drops of water to a sample of collodion, and it will generally remedy the defect. If the defect is removed in a small quantity, add water to the whole.

RETOUCHING NEGATIVES FOR PHOTOGRAPHIC VIEWS.

In photograph views, the sky is not usually very truthfully represented. It almost always appears too dark when representing a thunder tempest, or when the landscape, or whatever may be taken, betrays a shining sun. This unnatural effect may be overcome in the following manner:—The black varnish which is used for Ambrotypes, can be reduced by the addition of spirits of turpentine, and with a small brush spread it over the entire sky. If it still prints too dark, give it another coat; and if a white is desired, the negative must be made entirely opaque.

Beautiful clouds and sunset effects may be introduced into the photographic landscape, and at the expense of very little time. The tempestuous storm, the dark and dismal cloud, with the vivid flash of lightning dancing upon its thundering bosom, the rainbow and other scenes of grandeur and beauty, may be represented in the photographic drawing.

RETOUCHING NEGATIVE PHOTOGRAPHS.

This is best accomplished with india ink, and some other lighter color to modify it; the black spots may be retouched to their proper transparency or opacity. Shadows, if too deep or too feeble, may be corrected; defects in the eye also, if shaded too deep, may be corrected by a careful hand, guided by the use of a small camel's-hair pencil.

ENGRAVING THE NAME UPON A NEGATIVE.

Any name may be engraved upon the negative by marking it carefully with a pointed instrument —such as a needle or the point of a knife—before it is varnished. When printed, this will appear very distinct.

IMPERFECTIONS COMMON TO NEGATIVES.

The more frequent imperfections are those termed fogging, streaking, and spotting of the negative plate.

The causes are—*over-exposure in the camera, over-developing, impure chemicals, and light gaining access to the chemical-room, camera, or plate-holder.*

The over-exposure in the camera is easily obviated by lessening the time. The over-developing can be obviated by lessening the time also, and weakening the developer—changing the quantity of acetic acid.

The impurity of the chemicals in the collodion can only be ascertained by having a sample of collodion known positively by previous experiment to be of the good quality. Make a trial of this, and compare results.

Light gaining access to the Chemical-room, Plate-holder, Camera, &c.—After coating the plate as usual in the dark room, hold it in your hand for a few moments; then, without taking it out to the light, pour on the developer. If the plate blackens, white light gains admission to your chemical-room. *Make it darker.* If the cause is not here, coat another plate, put it in the plateholder, place it in the camera, and, without taking the cap off the tube, raise the slide, and expose the plate for a few seconds in the darkened chamber of the camera—remove it to the dark room, and pour on the developer; if it blackens, stop the leaks in the camera. If this does not obviate the trouble, coat another plate, put it into the plateholder, place it in the camera, and, *without removing the cap or raising the slide,* leave it a few seconds as before; remove to the chemical-room, pour on the developer; if it blackens, the plateholder is not tight. These trials will generally disclose the cause of fogging.

Sometimes the cause may be removed by adding acetic acid to the bath when all other means fail. This is an excellent remedy for fogging generally, and will, in nine cases out of ten, obviate the difficulty.

Specks upon the Plate.—These may occur from the use of collodion holding small particles in suspension, or from too much acid in the developer. Never use a sample of collodion until it has stood long enough to settle perfectly clear. All new collodions must be set aside where they will be undisturbed twenty-four hours before using.

Oily Spots or Lines up and down the Plate.—These occur when the plate is taken out of the silver bath, before the ether and alcohol have been washed away. Marks of the same shape occur, also, when the developer does not amalgamate readily with the surface of the film; in which case add a little alcohol to the developer.

SILVERY APPEARANCE OF NEGATIVES.

Negatives sometimes have an appearance of silver under the collodion after developing, which is owing mainly to the imperfect cleaning of the plate. This is more likely to occur when old plates are used. To avoid this, use nitric acid diluted and rotten-stone in the next cleaning. Glass which is rusty will always present this silvery appearance. It must be discarded.

Transparent Markings of various Kinds.—These sometimes resemble fern-leaves, and other vegetable forms: add a few drops of chloroform to the collodion. Dark spots of various forms may be caused by the collodion setting too long—or by pouring on the developer entirely on one place—or by having the developer too strong. Apply the remedies before recommended.

THE STRENGTH OF THE NITRATE BATH.

The last and highly important imperfection is often caused by the want of silver in the bath. A weak bath is indicated by certain parts of the plate having the appearance of transparency, as though no collodion was upon its surface. Test the bath with the hydrometer to ascertain the quantity of silver, and add enough to render the quantity equal to that required for the collodion, to be used generally 50 grains to every ounce of water.

There are, perhaps, many other imperfections in the negative process, which, were they fully enumerated here, would tend most likely to mislead rather than give information.

It is hoped that the practice of the art, as laid down in the pages of this work, will not cause so many failures as will deter the persevering student; assured that although the process is fraught with difficulties, it has been entirely overcome by many successful artists, the evidence of which is afforded by their works.

HINTS AND SUGGESTIONS IN PRINTING POSITIVES ON PAPER—PHOTOGRAPHIC PAPER.

The quality of paper is very important, and must be of an even texture, and free from holes and spots when held up to transmitted light. One side must have a satin appearance when viewed at an angle across the surface.

There is one side only of good photographic paper which will receive the best impression, and that may be known by examining it carefully. The one side will appear to have lines crossing, each resembling fibres in woven cloth. The opposite side will appear to show like satin, which is the one to receive the silver.

Avoid dust in the room where the paper is silvered and hung up to dry. Especially be careful to exclude it from the silvering solutions by frequent filtering.

WASHING POSITIVE PRINTS.

In washing positive prints great care must be observed that the dishes used are free from any foreign substance, as that would invariably cause spots or stains. The dishes mostly in use are gutta-percha or vulcanized india-rubber. With large prints, wooden dishes may be used if they are well varnished with gum shellac varnish, as described on page 191. The use of warm water to finish the washing is highly recommended, as in that state the hyposulphite of silver is much more soluble.

The value of the use of the chloride of gold in the toning bath has never been sufficiently estimated. It adds to the tone all the beauty so much desired. An increase of the quantity in the toning bath will frequently overcome the many disagreeable colors which are so often found in prints after washing. Its use in the finish of the Daguerreotype was considered indispensable. Those who seek for the most beautiful Photographs must use large quantities of this metallic salt.

RETOUCHING PHOTOGRAPHS.

All Photographs, when mounted, can be improved by slightly retouching them with a small camel's-hair brush dipped in india-ink. Especially the eyes, lips, &c., which frequently will not print clear and distinct. The ink can be ground on a piece of glass, using only a small quantity at a time. By mixing a small portion of carmine with the india-ink, any shade may be produced to correspond with the color of the print, and all the white spots that so frequently appear on the background and drapery can be removed. A slight touching of the ink on the shadows of the nostrils and lips will add greatly to the beauty of the Photograph.

Should any black spots require removal, use white water-color paint mixed with india-ink. This retouching will require only a short time, and must be done before varnishing.

IMPERFECTIONS FOUND IN POSITIVES ON PAPER.

If the print has a faded and yellow appearance, the hyposulphite is acid, or too old and weak; or the print has been left in it too long a time, or has been washed too slowly. Add more chloride of gold; if acid (which may be known by testing with litmus paper), add a few drops of aqua ammonia.

If not sufficient contrast exists between the lights and shadows, the print being pale, and without vigor, then the nitrate of silver solution is too weak in proportion to the salt solution. Strengthen the silver solution.

If too much contrast exists between the lights and the shadows, and the details are not marked in the latter, then increase the proportion of salt.

If pale spots appear, then there has been insufficient absorption of the nitrate of silver by the paper; this may result from the unequal texture of the paper, or from the silver being too weak.

Black spots are caused by dust on the surface of the silver solution, organic matter on the paper, or metallic particles in the paper. Be careful to avoid them.

If the prints after drying have a mottled appearance in the high lights, they have not been sufficiently toned. The prints should always be held up and examined by transmitted light before removing them from the toning bath.

If the bath is too weak, these spots cannot be removed except by adding more hyposulphite and chloride of gold to the bath.

These imperfections noticed as found in positive pictures on paper, probably do not include all, but those which are most likely to be encountered in the practice of the art. They are given as material for reference during the practical operations of the photographer, and should be often referred to in his leisure moments.

THE AMBROTYPE MANUAL.

PART II.

PRACTICAL DETAILS

OF THE

AMBROTYPE PROCESS.

POSITIVE PHOTOGRAPHS ON GLASS.

CHAPTER VIII.

THE CAMERA—PLATE-HOLDERS NECESSARY FOR THE CAMERA—PREPARING THE GLASSES—PLATE BLOCKS FOR HOLDING THE GLASSES—CLEANING SUBSTANCES—CLEANING THE GLASSES—CLEANING OLD GLASSES—REMOVING THE VARNISH—HOLDING GLASSES AFTER THEY ARE CLEANED—GLASSES USED A NUMBER OF TIMES—QUALITY OF GLASSES NECESSARY FOR AMBROTYPES

It is presumed that most persons in whose hands this book may fall, or at least those who see it after having sought it, are acquainted with the Daguerreotype process, and possess a camera, and all the apparatus necessary for Daguerreotypes. It is needless to add to those who have had any experience, that a good camera is indispensable, much more so than in the Daguerreian process. Without this necessary auxiliary, all labor will be but in vain.

An entirely new plate-holder for the camera is requisite, known as photographic frames, for holding the glass. It is made in such a manner that the glass plate will rest on each corner on glass itself. These holders are absolutely indispensable, because all attempts to use the old Daguerreian plate-holders will invariably produce bad results. These plate-holders can be obtained of any of the dealers in materials for the art.

The glasses, of course, have sharp edges, which may be filed off with a coarse file, or ground on a grindstone, to avoid cutting the fingers in handling. The wooden vise, which has been so often used for Peck's patent blocks, will answer a very good purpose for holding the glasses while cleaning them. It is better to procure two such vises—one for the acid and rottenstone, and the other for the alcohol.

The place where the ends of the glasses rest may be slightly raised, so that in passing the canton-flannel, or buff, over the glass, it shall pass entirely over the end or sides.

The plate vise may be dispensed with, and a flat pine board may be used, covered with canton-flannel, of a size longer than the glasses that are to be cleaned. On the edge of this board must be nailed a narrow piece of hard wood, raised just above the edge, but not so high as the thickness of the glass to be cleaned. Now, by pressing the glass against this edge with a small stick of hard wood, or the left hand, the glasses will be held, and readily cleaned with the other.

New glasses require cleaning first only with alcohol, or with alcohol and rottenstone. Common whiting has been found to answer the purpose even better than rottenstone. They are to be rubbed with canton-flannel, or tissue-paper, and then dried with the same substances. The plate must be rubbed in lines, round and round, and on both sides. It does not require as long rubbing as the Daguerreotype plate. After which, it is necessary to buff them with two buffs, like a ball covered with soft buckskin. This ball may be made of cotton, and covered with buckskin, with a handle made of the ends of the skin, drawn over, and tied with a piece of twine. The first ball, or *tampon*, may be rubbed with rouge, or rouge and calcined lampblack. The second is to be kept free from all polishing substances. Rub first with the rouge buff, and finish quickly with the dry one. By slightly breathing on the surface, one can readily ascertain if the plate is clean, which will be indicated by a uniform condensation of the moisture. Both sides of the glasses should be rubbed; also the edges of all should be wiped with a small piece of canton-flannel, before using, to remove any of the polishing substances which might adhere to the glasses.

Glasses which have impressions on them, and are dried, should first be placed in a flat dish containing water, or water and nitric acid, enough to make the liquid act slightly on the silver. They are then to be rubbed with rottenstone, or whiting, mixed with water and nitric acid—about two drachms of acid to four ounces of water. They are then to be thoroughly washed with pure water, and allowed to stand a few moments, or they may be immediately wiped dry with a clean towel. They are now ready for the alcohol and the canton-flannel process, which is effected without any application of rottenstone or whiting, although a small quantity of either may be used with the alcohol.

After the plates are buffed, they may be placed on their edges in some old plate-boxes which have done service in the Daguerreian art. The grooves can be cut out a little wider than those for plates, and then placed on the shelves near the bath, or laid on the edges ready for coating.

Old pictures which have been fitted up with the various varnishes require more care in cleaning.

They should be first placed in a strong solution of spirits of turpentine and alcohol, and allowed to remain there until the varnish becomes softened. Then they should be submitted to the acid and rottenstone, and finished in the same manner as glasses with pictures without varnish. It is well to place all pictures which are failures in water as soon as possible, rather than to allow them to dry with the collodion on them.

The towel used for wiping the glasses should be used only for that purpose, and no soap, or any other substance, should be allowed to soil it. When washed, it should be only with soda, instead of soap, to insure more complete success.

The glasses should always be kept away from any dampness and dust. Great care must be taken that no vapors of chemicals should come in contact with glasses after they are cleaned. Other substances may be employed, such as tripoli powder, photogene, &c., care being taken to remove all the polishing substances before the plate goes into the bath.

Glasses, unlike Daguerreotype plates, may be cleaned and used a great number of times; but they will require more careful polishing after a few impressions are made, and it has even been asserted by some operators that they will actually loose their sensitiveness after a few trials. It is well, therefore, not to use the glasses too long; yet the practice is so variable, that some kinds of glass may answer, whilst others may be useless.

The finest quality of plate glass is best adapted for Ambrotypes, and that which is free from color will produce the most pleasing effects. Many persons, however, use an inferior quality of glass, which of course is a great detriment to their pictures. The thickness of the glass is of some consequence. It should not be too thick, else the picture will appear unnatural. A medium thickness is to be obtained, if possible.

CHAPTER IX.

APPARATUS FOR AMBROTYPES—CHEMICALS USED—SUBSTANCES FOR FINISHING THE PICTURE—PREPARATION OF THE NITRATE BATH—TO IODIZE THE BATH—FILTERING PROCESS—ADDING ACID—NEUTRALIZING THE BATH—FULL DIRECTIONS FOR KEEPING THE BATH IN ORDER—RENEWAL OF THE NITRATE OF SILVER.

The following are the various utensils, or apparatus, necessary for the Ambrotype process:

APPARATUS.

One gutta-percha bath.
One dipping rod—glass or gutta-percha.
One flat dish for fixing solution, either of earthenware or gutta-percha—the latter preferred.
One large earthen dish for the developing solution.
One bottle for the developing solution, capable of holding two quarts.
One four, or six ounce graduated glass.
One large bottle, with a glass stopper, capable of holding more than the silver bath, and to be used *exclusively* for that purpose.
Three glass or gutta-percha funnels, to be used respectively for the nitrate of silver, the developing solution, and the fixing bath.

One actino-hydrometer, for testing the nitrate bath.

A new and distinct plate-frame, for holding the glass plates when placed in the camera.

One pair of scales, containing apothecaries' and avoirdupois weights.

Cotton for filtering.

Two or three glass rods.

The following chemicals will be found necessary:

CHEMICALS.

Nitrate of silver (crystallized).	Iodized collodion.*
Protosulphate of iron.	Nitric acid, chemically pure.
Acetic acid.	Glacial acetic acid.
Alcohol 95 per cent.	Litmus-paper, blue and red.
Cyanide of potassium.	Iodide of potassium.
Hyposulphite of soda.	Carbonate of soda.

The following substances are required to finish the picture:

REQUISITES FOR FINISHING.

White varnish.	Gum demar varnish.
Black varnish.	Venetian or Canada balsam.
Amber varnish.	Daguerreotype sealing-paper.

Being supplied with all the various utensils and chemicals, the first and most important preparation would be the nitrate of silver bath, and herein

---

* The preparation of the collodion will be found in Chapter XI.

lies one of the main secrets of success in all the practice. Unless the bath be properly prepared at the outset, with all care in manipulating and in the compounding of the other chemicals, all the productions will be failures.

The bath once in a proper state, success is much more easily attained.

First measure the bath by filling it with water, then pouring it into the graduated glass to ascertain the exact number of fluid ounces which the bath contains. To every ounce of water in the bath must be added forty grains of nitrate of silver, pure and crystallized, and free from acid. Test a small quantity of nitrate of silver in solution with blue litmus-paper. If any acid is present, the paper instantly becomes red.

By calculation the quantity required for the bath can easily be ascertained, as there are 480 grains to every ounce. If the bath contains two quarts, or 64 ounces, it will require exactly 2,560 grains, or $5\frac{1}{3}$ ounces of the nitrate of silver. Thus:

$$64 \times 40 = 2560 \div 480 = 5\frac{1}{3} \text{ ounces.}$$

Procure distilled water in all cases, if possible; but if this be not always obtainable, pure soft water, which has been boiled and filtered, may answer. In no case use water that has any trace of lime or soda.

As a test of pure water may not always be at hand, it is well to take a few grains of nitrate of silver, and drop it into an ounce of the water before using. Should it appear to dissolve, or throw down any precipitate, you may be assured that the quality is not good, and it will not answer for the bath.

Dissolve all the silver, except one ounce, in the water, which must be placed in the large glass-stoppered bottle appropriated expressly for the bath, reserving, also, about four or six ounces of the water intended for the bath, which may be placed in the graduated glass. Into this put the extra ounce of nitrate of silver, and dissolve.

TO MAKE THE IODIDE OF SILVER FOR THE BATH.

Take about twelve grains of iodide of potassium, and dissolve it in one ounce of water, and add to it two drachms of the nitrate of silver solution from the large bottle. Avoid strong daylight in this process. Immediately there will be seen a yellow precipitate, which is the iodide of silver. This must now be well washed three or four times with soft water, by adding eight or ten ounces at a time, and allowing it to subside, when the superfluous water must be poured off; then add fresh water until all the potassium is washed out, leaving the pure iodide of silver.

This iodide of silver is now to be poured into the six ounces of water in which one ounce of nitrate of silver was dissolved. Stir it with a glass rod, and after it is partially dissolved, pour the whole into the large bottle containing the solution for the bath; shake it well, and filter through the funnel expressly reserved for the nitrate bath.

This amount of iodide of silver will be required for a bath containing two quarts. The same proportions must be observed for baths of other dimensions.

FILTERING PROCESS.

The best filter is composed of clean cotton, which must first be saturated with alcohol, and afterwards thoroughly washed out with water. This filter is preferable to all others for photographic purposes; and in all cases where filtering is required, it is strongly recommended.

The color of the bath should at first appear to be a milky hue, but after filtering once or twice (as may be necessary), it should be clear as water There will be a portion of the iodide of silver which will not be dissolved. This must in all cases be filtered out, and the solution rendered perfectly clear before it is ready for use.

After the bath is clear, test it with the hydrometer made expressly for the purpose, to ascertain if it be of the required strength—viz., forty grains to the ounce, which will be indicated on the scale graduated according to the table in the book accompanying the hydrometer.

The bath must also be tested with blue litmus-paper, by cutting off a small slip, and dropping one end of it into the solution. If it turns red, you have already a portion of acid.

A small quantity of acid is necessary to produce the required tone and effect of the collodion, and also to remove any streaks that may sometimes present themselves.

Two kinds are used, chemically pure—viz., nitric and glacial acetic acid. The former has been said to produce the finest white tones, yet it is more liable to change the nature of the bath, while the latter is said to possess a more uniform action, and to work with great regularity.

The quantity used, however, of either is very

small—not over eight or ten drops to be added at first. Should lines appear running up and down the plate, five or six drops more may be added. Of course only one kind of acid is to be used at a time.

TO NEUTRALIZE THE NITRATE OF SILVER BATH.

In order to neutralize the bath, dissolve half an ounce of carbonate of soda in two ounces of water; then pour into the solution a drachm or two at a time, quickly shaking the bottle. The bath will assume a whitish appearance, which will disappear on shaking the bottle. When a sufficient quantity of the soda has been added to neutralize all the acid, this whitish appearance will remain after shaking the bottle. As soon as that is seen, there can be no more soda added without injury to the bath. Try the litmus-paper, and when enough soda has been added, it will of course remain unchanged.

Sometimes caustic potash is employed to neutralize the bath, when a brown precipitate falls, instead of a white. If nitric acid has been used, and one desires to employ the glacial acetic instead, it can be easily neutralized by the foregoing process, and the latter acid added.

Sometimes a perfectly neutral bath will succeed well in the Ambrotype process, and it is even recommended at first to be used in that state before adding the acid—the acid being added only when the lines make their appearance on the plate.

The bath should always be kept as much excluded from the light as possible, and also covered, to avoid collecting dust and other foreign substances. It may remain constantly in the gutta-percha dish without serious injury. Many operators prefer pouring it into the bottle after the labors of the day, both for safety from accident, and also on the score of cleanliness.

Avoid the introduction of any vegetable or metallic substance into the bath, or the slightest particle of alkaline ingredient, in any form. It frequently happens that particles of collodion will leave the plate, and be found floating in the bath. Whenever this occurs, it is necessary to filter it.

The gutta-percha bath should be arranged in a square box or frame, at an angle of about thirty degrees, or, what is better still, a covered box, that should open when desired, and cover the whole when not in use. A dark cloth may also be employed to cover it.

There should always be a sufficient quantity of

the nitrate of silver solution reserved in the large bottle to keep the bath full during the time of operating. An ounce of nitrate of silver, or a less quantity, may be dissolved in the bottle, without the addition of the iodide of silver, as in the first preparation of the bath.

Some operators flow their bath only in the morning, in order to remove the dust which collects on the surface, and would fix itself on the first plate introduced were it not so removed.

Avoid the contact of the human hands with the nitrate bath, as every drop leaves an indelible stain.

It is recommended to obtain a box which will support the plate-holder in an upright position after the plate is in it, previous to being placed in the focus of the camera, thereby avoiding damage to the floor or carpet upon which the camera stands.

A nitrate bath once prepared according to the foregoing plan, and in good working order, will remain in action for years, by adding occasionally a little more acid, say ten drops at a time, when lines appear, and nitrate of silver when required. After using a bath for a great number of impressions, it will be necessary to add more iodide of silver, which must be done in the same manner as described on page 134.

When the bath requires a renewal of the nitrate of silver, as it necessarily will, after a given quantity of plates have been prepared, the impressions will appear to be covered unevenly with silver, after the application of the fixing solution.

Test the bath with the hydrometer, and add more silver to bring the strength up to the requisite standard—viz., forty grains to each ounce of water.

CHAPTER X.

THE DEVELOPING SOLUTIONS—MANNER OF COMPOUNDING THEM—VARIOUS FORMULAS FOR DEVELOPING SOLUTIONS—TEST OF ACETIC ACID—THE FIXING SOLUTIONS—CYANIDE OF POTASSIUM—HYPOSULPHITE OF SODA—ADDING CHLORIDE OF SILVER.

THE DEVELOPING SOLUTION.

The chemicals used in the developing solution are sulphate of iron, acetic acid, and alcohol.

℞. Sulphate of iron, ... 2 ounces.
Acetic acid, No. 8, ... 2 ounces.
Alcohol (either 80 or 95 per cent.), . 1 ounce.
Water, ... 1 quart.

The sulphate of iron should be of pure quality, which may be known by its clear and transparent green crystals.

Dissolve the iron and water, and filter; then add the acetic acid and alcohol, keeping it in a glass-stoppered bottle, ready for use. Use it by pouring out a small quantity at a time in an open mouthed bottle, which will contain six or eight ounces.

Some prefer to add the acetic acid and alcohol, preserving the same proportions in the same bottle as it is required for use.

If one is not consuming it very rapidly, this latter plan is recommended.

It has been found, when all the ingredients are mixed at once, that the developing solution becomes changed after standing a few days, and a precipitate is formed.

In order to facilitate the dissolving of the sulphate of iron, it may be pulverized in a mortar, and warm water added instead of cold.

This solution is to be used only once upon the plate, as it forms with the silver another substance, which, on a second application, would injure the picture. Some operators, however, have filtered and used it again by adding a small quantity of acetic acid.

There are other solutions and other formulas for the developer which are highly recommended, a few of which are given:

No. 1. Proto-sulphate of iron, . . 2 ounces.
Acetic acid, No. 8, . . 2 ounces.
Alcohol, ... 1 ounce.
Nitric acid, ... ½ ounce.
Water, ... 1 quart.

IMPURITIES OF ACETIC ACID. 143

No. 2. Proto-sulphate of iron, . . 4 ounces.
       Acetic acid, No. 8, . . . 4 ounces.
       Alcohol, ... 4 ounces.
       Water, ... 1 quart.

No. 3. Proto-sulphate of iron, . . 3 ounces.
       Acetic acid, No. 8, . . . 3 ounces.
       Alcohol, ... 3 ounces.
       Sulphuric acid, ... ½ ounce.
       Water, ... 1 quart.

No. 4. Proto-sulphate of iron, . . 1 ounce.
       Nitrate of potash (refined nitre), . ¾ ounce.
       Acetic acid, ... 3 ounces.
       Water, ... 1 quart.

The foregoing receipts are given mainly to indicate the various processes, all tending to the same results. The addition of nitric acid and sulphuric acid has been said by some to render the pictures whiter. But this is doubted by others; and the result of a long experience has shown that the first receipt here given will produce the best pictures.

There are many impurities of acetic acid, and it is necessary to test it, which is done by putting merely one or two drachms of the silver solution from the bath into a small quantity of the acid, or either dissolve a small quantity of nitrate of silver, and add it to the acid. If the acid exhibits any precipitate, it will not answer for the purposes of a developing agent.

THE FIXING SOLUTIONS.

The fixing solutions are composed of cyanide of potassium and hyposulphite of soda, as follows:

No. 1. Cyanide of potassium, . . . ½ ounce.
        Water, ... 1 pint.

Dissolve and filter, and it is ready for use.

No. 2. Hyposulphite of soda, . . 4 ounces.
        Water, ... 1 pint.

Dissolve and filter.

The fixing solutions are very simple, and easily kept in order, except that, after using for a number of pictures, they will require strengthening.

Some operators add a small quantity of chloride of silver to the solution, and it is said it will render the pictures of a whiter and purer tone.

Filter this solution often, and avoid dust and other foreign substances.

The cyanide of potassium fixing solution is the one greatly preferred, and most commonly used for the Ambrotype process.

CHAPTER XI.

ON THE PRACTICE OF THE ART IN ALL ITS DETAILS, FROM THE CLEANING OF THE PLATE TO THE APPLICATION OF THE FIXING SOLUTION—DRYING THE PICTURE.

The practice of this art is such, that a careful and accurate manner of the manipulating through the whole is necessary to insure success.

It is absolutely necessary to have a dark room, or one that can be made so at will, and yet a lamp or candle will be required in some portion of the process, or if a window is arranged with a yellow reflection within the room by yellow cloth or reflectors it will answer as well. The lamp should be placed behind a yellow glass, so that whatever light falls upon the glass plate shall be of a yellow hue, as the plate is very sensitive to the light on its removal from the bath. By some operators it is asserted that all these precautions are not necessary.

The plate glass is first to be cleaned thoroughly,

according to the directions in a former portion of this work. It is then well brushed off with a soft camel's-hair brush, in order to remove all the dust.

Standing near the bath with your collodion well decanted, as described in the section of this work devoted to collodion, holding the glass in your left-hand thumb and finger, pour out very carefully a continuous stream of collodion upon the middle of the plate, sufficient in quantity when allowed to flow entirely over, to cover it entirely.

Allow the collodion to flow first to the lower left-hand corner, then to the lower right-hand, and finally let the superfluous quantity return into the bottle at the right-hand corner near the thumb. A little practice will enable one to pour the collodion on the glass, and return that portion not required to the bottle without waste.

Avoid any contact of the collodion with the thumb, as streaks will be caused thereby; but if a portion should run on the opposite side of the glass, it will not injure the picture, as that can be easily removed after it is taken from the fixing solution.

Hold the plate nearly horizontal with the daylight on it, so that the light shall reflect on the surface of the glass, and always retain the position of it down, in the same manner as it was when the collodion was poured into the bottle from the glass—that is, the end where the collodion left the plate must always be kept lower than the other portion. As soon as the film appears to be drying, as it will in a few seconds, and when, by just placing the finger on a corner of the plate, the collodion becomes of a glutinous nature, or, rather, as soon as it is set, immerse it in your bath, with the same lower portion of the plate down as when you were setting the film.

The plate should never be entirely dry, but hold a medium between moisture and dryness. The light must now be excluded from the bath, either by covering it with a dark cloth, or closing the box containing the bath, or the door of the room, and the plate allowed to remain in the bath one or two minutes. It may then be carefully raised from the bath, and if a film of iodide of silver is formed suflicient for its removal to the camera, it will assume a perfectly smooth appearance on viewing the surface; but if the glass is removed too soon, it will have the appearance of grease, and run in lines down the plate.

In order to facilitate the process, you can move the glass slightly from side to side in your bath, raising it carefully, and viewing the surface, or the plate may remain in the bath three or four minutes, during which time the person whose likeness is to be taken may be placed in position.

On removing the plate from the bath, care should be observed that no daylight falls upon it. The nitrate of silver should be allowed to run off for a few seconds into the bath before placing it in photographic frames. After the plate is in the frames ready for the camera, it must always remain in a perpendicular position, leaning against the wall, or some other substance. Never allow it to be placed horizontally from the moment the glass is in the frame until it is developed, or lines will be produced on the plate. Before the next plate is placed in the frame, it must be carefully wiped dry with a dry cloth or towel.

As short a time as possible should elapse after the glass is in the plate-holder before placing it in the focus of the camera. The time required in the camera, of course, must be determined by actual experiment.

The plate is then taken to the developing stand, which must be so arranged that water can flow on the plate at any moment, after pouring on the developing solution. Holding the plate again in the left hand, as in using the collodion, over a large dish sufficient to receive all the solution that will not remain on the surface, quickly pour over the developing solution on the right-hand side of the glass, enough to cover it all at the same instant, and move it over the whole surface, as in gilding a Daguerreotype plate. The picture will quickly appear; and as soon as the outlines of the drapery are seen distinctly, then apply the water to the surface in a gentle stream, so as not to remove the collodion film.

A little care and experience will be necessary in the developing process, for in this consists the great beauty of the picture. By a proper development all the fine half tints are produced, and the drapery is brought out with distinctness.

It is preferred by some rather to over-time the picture in the camera, and use a shortened developing process, yet the best results are attained by the exact time of exposure, combined with the proper development. It is well known that the longer the picture is developed, the lighter it becomes; but beyond a certain length of time, a disagreeable tone is produced. It is necessary, therefore, to allow sufficient time in the camera for the picture to be developed in the usual manner.

About ten or fifteen seconds, in ordinary temperature, is long enough for a successful development. This, however, is subject to a variety of changes, which must be learned by actual experience.

After thoroughly washing the solution from the glass on both sides, lay it in a flat dish containing the fixing solution, with the collodion side uppermost. This may be performed in the light of day. If cyanide of potassium is used, it will remove the iodide of silver which has been unchanged by the action of the light in a few seconds. But if hyposulphate is used, it will require somewhat longer. As soon as the picture is seen clearly, be careful to remove it, to wash all the fixing solution from the glass with a good supply of soft water, as the slightest trace of these solutions will injure the picture.

The plate can now be dried by a gentle heat of the fire, but not too quickly, as streaks will be formed. It is now ready for the varnishes.

The glasses may also be dried by the application of the spirit-lamp, care being used to avoid too great heat, which will cause the glass to break.

CHAPTER XII.

VARNISHING THE PICTURE—SINGLE GLASS PROCESS—STEREOSCOPIC AMBROTYPE—TREBLE GLASS PROCESS—THE DOUBLE GLASS PROCESS—CUTTING'S PATENT—THE PATENT LEATHER PROCESS.

There are so many kinds of varnishes in use, and such a variety of modes of sealing up the Ambrotypes, that one is in great doubt which is best to be adopted. We shall give all the various plans adopted by the profession, including the great process, known as Cutting's patent.

SINGLE GLASS PROCESS.

The plan mostly adopted of applying the varnishes, is to pour them on like the collodion.

All pictures which are put up with the single glasses are said to be improved by the application of the white varnish before the black is used; yet by some it is asserted they are the same after the black is applied as though no white had been ap plied. The white varnish will dry very soon if the plate is slightly warmed by the spirit-lamp, when the black can be added, and allowed to dry by laying it in a horizontal position, with the varnish uppermost.

The black varnish can be applied directly on the collodion side, without the white varnish.

In most instances the black varnish has a tendency to darken the picture—hence the picture when dried and ready for the varnish should appear rather lighter than you desire it when finished.

Pictures can also be varnished with the white varnish on the collodion side, and the black on the opposite side. These can be colored as in a Daguerreotype plate, and sealed up with a mat and glass in the same manner. They are sometimes colored before the white varnish is applied. Many are sealed up with the collodion side colored, and not varnished with the white, but only black, on the reverse side.

STEREOSCOPIC AMBROTYPES.

There is quite a novel method of sealing Ambrotypes, by some called stereoscopic, because they have a stereoscopic effect, even without the stereoscopic lenses. The Ambrotype is first taken with a dark background, instead of the usual white one. After it is dried, a small camel's-hair brush is used to apply the black varnish to the reverse side of the glass, and only enough to cover the figure, and allowing the background to remain perfectly clear and transparent. Place a piece of white paper, or, what is better, Bristol board, on the back of the glass, and the picture will be seen to stand out from the background in relief.

All the pictures sealed with the collodion side uppermost will require a glass over them for protection.

TREBLE GLASS PROCESS.

By using a third glass instead of the white paper, a beautiful effect is produced, if the glass is coated with collodion, and exposed in the camera to the white background, and developed and fixed exactly as in the process of taking the portrait. Any desired shade can be attained, and a great variety of colors may be used, instead of white, the effect of which is very pleasing.

Another beautiful effect may be produced by first taking a view from some engraving of scenery, &c.—coloring it, and using that for the third or back glass.

DOUBLE GLASS PROCESS.

The use of Canada balsam in sealing up Ambrotypes has been adopted by those who have heretofore used the "*cutting*" process. The balsam has been found on trial to be very difficult of application, and perplexing. The adoption of good white varnish instead is much preferable, being attended with less than half the trouble, and rendering the pictures more clear and transparent.

They can be colored on the collodion side, and put up with the transparent case with great facility.

The varnish, however, should be a little thicker than ordinary white varnish, which can be rendered so by exposing it for a day or two to the open air, or the addition of a little more gum copal will answer the same end.

Only a small quantity need be used, say one or two drops on the middle of the glass. Gently press the second glass upon the varnish, and it will immediately flow over the whole surface. The picture can be sealed with the sealing-paper before it has flowed over entirely, which will prevent the superfluous varnish from running out at the sides of the glasses.

Any white gums may be dissolved either in spirits of turpentine or alcohol, and used for the medium of holding the two glasses; but the common white varnishes have been found to answer quite as well as the Canada balsam.

PATENT LEATHER PROCESS.

Ambrotypes can be easily transferred from the glass plate to the surface of patent leather by the following process:

Add thirty drops of nitric acid to two ounces of alcohol, and after the picture is well dried upon the glass, pour enough of the alcohol, prepared as above, on the surface to cover it.

Clean the japanned surface of the patent leather with soft canton flannel only, and pour over the alcohol two or three times. Then lay the leather upon the surface of the picture, and place another glass over it, retaining the leather between the two glasses with the patent clothes-pins, or in any manner to press the glasses evenly over the leather, for about ten minutes; they can then be separated, and the picture will leave the glass and adhere to the leather, which, when dried, can be rubbed without any possibility of removal.

APPLYING THE CANADA BALSAM.

In applying the Canada balsam, or any thickened varnish, between the glasses, great care should be used in pouring it on the surface of the glass. It must be placed on the middle of the glass plate, say about two or three drops, and the additional glass carefully cleaned, and free from dust, laid over first on one edge, then to be pressed gently down, and before the balsam spreads out to the edges, it can be sealed up with the adhesive paper. It will in a short time spread entirely over the surface, and render the picture clear and transparent.

The application of the balsam is necessarily attended with more difficulty than any other varnishes which are recommended, from its peculiar glutinous properties, and the tendency it has to ooze out at the edges after the picture is sealed. It can, however, be removed effectually by alcohol, and rubbing it with canton-flannel, as all the balsams and gums are soluble in strong 95 per cent. alcohol.

CHAPTER XIII.

THE MANUFACTURE OF GUN-COTTON—TEST OF THE ACIDS EMPLOYED—WASHING AND DRYING THE GUN-COTTON—PREPARATION OF THE COLLODION—ITS NATURE AND PROPERTIES—ETHER AND ALCOHOL—TO IODIZE COLLODION FOR AMBROTYPES—METHOD OF PRESERVING COLLODION, AND KEEPING IT READY FOR USE—TESTS OF GOOD COLLODION—TO REMOVE THE COLOR FROM COLLODION.

A WORK like this would be incomplete without full and practical details relative to the preparation of gun-cotton, and its conversion into collodion, although the manufacture of it is attended with considerable difficulty and uncertainty. It is recommended to beginners, therefore, to purchase their collodion of those more experienced operators, when only a small quantity is required. Indeed, the manufacture of gun-cotton itself is liable to great variation, as well as being very deleterious to health. It is found that even those who make collodion for sale, purchase their gun-cotton ready made. Both gun-cotton and collodion are all perfectly iodized and warranted. They can be found for sale by most dealers in Daguerreotype goods.

Collodion is so called from a Greek word, which signifies "to stick." It is a transparent fluid, procured generally by dissolving gun-cotton in ether, or ether and alcohol.

It was discovered by Professor Schöenbein, of Basle, Switzerland, in the year 1846, and was first used for surgical purposes only, being smeared over fresh wounds and raw surfaces, in order to preserve them from contact with the air by the tough film which it leaves on evaporation. It is now sold by druggists for the same purpose; but photographers have hailed the discovery of collodion as the final keystone to their wonderful art, and they draw large contributions from this substance. It is consequently of great importance that its preparation should be the most complete and exact that can be attained.

Gun-cotton is procured by immersing the pure clean fibres of cotton in sulphuric acid and nitric acid, or sulphuric acid and nitrate of potash.

If a large quantity of gun-cotton is desired, the mixture of nitric and sulphuric acid is generally adopted. For photographic purposes, however, the mixture of nitrate of potash and sulphuric acid is used as follows:

TO MAKE GUN-COTTON.

Granulated nitrate of potash,	6 ounces.
Sulphuric acid,	5 ounces.
Pure cotton,	160 grains.

The nitrate of potash should be pulverized in a porcelain mortar, and the sulphuric acid added and mixed until a thick pasty substance is formed, when the cotton must be quickly immersed, and stirred with a glass rod, so as to thoroughly incorporate the cotton in the mixture. Then pound the cotton slightly for a period of ten minutes. When the cotton assumes a stringy appearance, and on separating the fibres, it breaks easily, it must be quickly immersed in a quantity of water to remove the acid, after which it is to be well washed for ten or fifteen minutes in water, constantly changing it, until all traces of the acid disappear. Great care is necessary to be observed in preparing the gun-cotton. It should be made in an open space, where free circulation of air is obtained, in order that the deleterious fumes of the acid shall pass away. The quality of the ingredients is highly essential. The rectified nitrate of potash, known as "Dupont's granulated nitre," is preferable. The acid should be of the specific gravity of 1.860, and free from water.

On mixing the acid and nitre, the temperature should be raised to about 140°, or it will become so if they are of the required quality, in consequence of the small quantity of water contained in the nitre.

The most expeditious plan to wash the acid out is to have running water, as from a hydrant.

As soon as the acid is completely washed out, which may be ascertained positively by using litmus-paper, the cotton is then to be placed in alcohol, in order to remove all traces of water; then by wringing it out in a clean towel, all the alcohol can be removed, and it is then ready to spread out on white paper to dry, which will be done in a few moments.

If the manufacture of the gun-cotton, as above described, has been successful, the product will be capable of the following conditions: A small quantity will explode on the application of heat. It will dissolve readily in a solution of alcohol and ether, in certain proportions, without leaving much residuum.

PREPARATION OF COLLODION.

The manufacture of gun-cotton is usually attended with many difficulties, and liable in all cases to result in failure from the slightest variation of the process, and withal is quite detrimental to health. It is therefore recommended to purchase the gun-cotton, when possible, thereby saving all the perplexity and uncertainty attending its preparation.

PREPARATION OF THE COLLODION.

Assured that you have a good quality of gun-cotton, the preparation of the plain collodion is attended with very little difficulty. The proportions are as follows:

Sulphuric ether, concentrated, sp. g. 720 . 10 ounces.
Alcohol, 95 per cent., sp. g. 820 . . 6 ounces.
Gun-cotton . . . . . . 80 grains.

Mix these in the order above given, and shake them thoroughly, when the cotton will be seen to dissolve, and the substance to assume a glutinous appearance on the inner surface of the bottle. In some instances it may require the addition of more gun-cotton to render the collodion of the required consistency. This can be ascertained by pouring a small quantity upon a piece of glass, and allowing the ether to evaporate. If a thick film is formed on the glass sufficient to hold together, and to be raised up without breaking very readily, it will answer; but if it does not contain these requisites, add more gun-cotton. If too thick, then add more ether and alcohol, in the same relative proportions.

Allow this to stand a few hours to settle, then decant into another bottle, leaving a small portion at the bottom, which will remain undissolved by the ether and alcohol. This sediment may be reserved until the next lot is required, and added to it without loss.

TO IODIZE THE COLLODION FOR AMBROTYPES.

Pure collodion,	8 ounces.
Bromo-iodide of silver,	4 drachms.

Prepared as described on page 185.

Hydro-bromic acid,	20 drops.

Prepared as described on page 187.

The iodizing of the collodion is also liable to a variety of uncertainties in the result. If there is any defect in the quality of the ether or the alcohol, the collodion will not work with good results. This can only be known on trial. If the film should not prove thick enough on using, add 20 grains of iodide of potassium and 10 grains of bromide of potassium, as follows: First dissolve the bromide in a drachm or two of water, then add the iodide. When both are well dissolved, add the whole to the eight ounces; shake it well, and allow it to stand for a few days. It will assume at first a thick and opaque appearance, but will settle clear, if left in quiet for a sufficient length of time for all the precipitate to fall. It can then be decanted into another bottle, ready for use.

The remainder of the collodion recipes, together with the preparations of the iodides and bromides, and the various saturated solutions, will be given in a separate chapter.

Collodion should be kept as much as possible from the light, although by some it is asserted that light does not affect its properties. Yet it must be apparent that if the collodion is affected by light in any form, it will certainly be if exposed to its rays for a long time. In no case should it be shaken after it is decanted.

The most successful manner of using collodion is to be provided with three long bottles made expressly for this purpose. Fill each one from the large bottle, allowing them to stand. Use from each bottle, alternately. By this means there can be no possibility of disturbing the particles in the collodion, and one will also avoid many spots and lines upon the glass plates.

Collodion requires to be perfectly clear and transparent in order to work successfully. The color may at times vary. On first mixing the ingredients, it will assume a yellow hue, changing to a darker shade, and finally to a red. The color does not in any degree affect the working properties of the collodion.

The tests of good collodion before working are, that it appears clear and transparent, devoid of small particles floating in it; that it be thick enough to form a film readily on the glass, and that it dries with perfect smoothness, without ridges or lines.

But the best test is to make a trial picture with it, and the result will soon convince one of the success or failure of his production.

TO REMOVE THE COLOR FROM COLLODION.

It may sometimes be necessary to remove the reddish color which is so often seen in Ambrotype collodion. In order to do this there can be added a few strips of zinc, or, what is more expeditious, add three or four ounces of pure mercury, and shake it well for a few moments, when the whole will assume a beautiful yellow color.

The mercury will subside, and the collodion may be poured off clear and transparent.

CHAPTER XIV.

COLORING AMBROTYPES—COLORS EMPLOYED—AMBROTYPES FOR LOCKETS—TAKING VIEWS—COPYING DAGUERREOTYPES BY THE AMBROTYPE PROCESS—COPYING ENGRAVINGS, STATUARY, MACHINERY, ETC.

The propriety of coloring the Ambrotype pictures has been questioned by many, and we may even doubt if they are improved by it; but many persons desire to see themselves in their *natural colors*. The artist is therefore compelled to devise some plan of gratifying the public taste, and color his pictures true to life.

Many attempts have been made to color Ambrotypes, and seal them with the single glass, with the colors to be seen, but this plan has been found impracticable, except in a certain degree. The colors may be seen through the glass if they are very deeply colored.

The black varnish removes nearly all color, even when it is placed over the white varnish, and the opacity of the collodion is such, also, that the colors themselves cannot be seen through the glass but very slightly, even before the black varnish is applied. The only feasible plan of applying the colors is on the collodion, blackening the reverse side of the glass. The colors are applied to the collodion after it is thoroughly dried, in the same manner as in the Daguerreotype; but it is necessary to color much more intensely, in order that the application of the white varnish may not remove all the color, as it invariably will a portion of it. After the white varnish is applied and dried, the picture can then be colored still more highly, if necessary, until the desired tint is acquired.

The colors which are best adapted for this purpose are not those commonly used for Daguerreotypes. The following are those which can be applied with the greatest facility, viz.:

   Chinese Vermillion.
   Chrome green.
   Chrome yellow.
   Chinese blue.
   Purple, a mixture of venetian red and blue.

The carmine used in the Daguerreotype will not adhere well to the Ambrotype, and the **substitu-**

tion of vermillion has been found to work exceedingly well, and to render the flesh color quite as natural as in the use of the carmine for the Daguerreotype.

The coloring of jewelry, &c., with moistened gold colors can be adapted to the collodion. With some improvement it will not be affected by the black varnish. The gilding is seen distinctly on either side of the picture; yet by some it is considered as being too conspicuous, and therefore discarded.

The application of most varnishes to the pictures after they are colored has a tendency to darken the whole of the light and shades. It will therefore be necessary to make the impression rather lighter than it is desired to have it when finished

Many operators put up their portraits after coloring, without applying the white varnish over the collodion, merely blackening the reverse side with black varnish.

It is not to be supposed that they are so durable, because the silver is liable, after a lapse of time, to become affected by the atmosphere, and it must necessarily change. All collodion pictures are of course much better protected by the application of varnish.

It frequently happens that the high lights on the hair of many Ambrotype portraits are too apparent, producing what is termed **gray hair.** This may be removed by a simple process, as follows:

Prepare some fine lampblack by holding a small piece of glass over an ordinary lamp. A black deposit will be formed of the finest lampblack. This can always be in readiness to darken the high lights; which is effected by a wet brush, with a small portion of this lampblack laid on where a darker shade is required.

AMBROTYPES FOR LOCKETS.

Portraits taken for lockets, breastpins, and medallions, by the Daguerreotype process, are easily inserted, but when taken on glass they are attended with much more difficulty.

A new and very useful invention has been made of a kind of plate, well adapted for locket pictures. They are known as the Melainotype plates, and are now employed by most operators for these kinds of pictures. Being composed of thin plates of iron, and japanned, they require no application of the black varnish, and can be cut and fitted into lockets with the same facility as Daguerreotypes.

Prepared paper is used by some operators for

these kinds of pictures, and patent-leather has been adopted by some. The process of taking them on patent-leather is given on page 155.

All these various materials can be purchased of the dealers in photographic materials.

FOR TRANSFERRING AMBROTYPES TO PAPER.

Gum-shellac	$1\frac{1}{2}$ ounce.
Borax	$\frac{1}{2}$ ounce.
Water	8 ounces.

Dissolve the borax in the water and add the shellac, which will require a slight degree of heat.

Use the black-glazed paper, cut a little larger than the glass on which the Ambrotype is taken. Pour a portion of this solution on the paper, and allow it to partially dry; then lay it over the Ambrotype, which must be well dried; and place the whole under water for five or ten minutes, when the paper can be removed with the picture upon its surface. Dry, and it is ready for use.

TAKING VIEWS BY THE AMBROTYPE PROCESS.

This is the most simple and easy process known in the art, because operators are always sure of a good light. The utility of it for taking views over that of the ordinary Daguerreotype will not be questioned when it is known that all objects are taken without reversing, and that, too, without the use of a reflector. The camera must be used with a small opening diaphragm, in order to reduce the light, and render the half tints discernible. The bath must be removed to some place near the object to be taken, because the plate will not be sensitive only as long as moisture remains on its surface. If many minutes should elapse after the impression is taken, it will be necessary to plunge the plate into the nitrate bath for a few seconds before applying the developer. It will then cause the picture to appear, even if it had been partially dried on its surface. As little time as possible should intervene after the impression is given before the developer is applied. All views must be sealed up with the black varnish applied to the collodion, otherwise they would appear reversed.

COPYING DAGUERREOTYPES BY THE AMBROTYPE PROCESS.

The durability of the Daguerreotype has long been doubted, yet many persons possess them which are in a good state of preservation, although taken ten or fifteen years ago.

But this new process of positive photographs on glass possesses advantages over the Daguerreotype that will command the preference on the score of durability. As this fact becomes more generally known, all those persons who possess a Daguerreotype of a departed friend, will hasten to the Ambrotype artist, and have it reproduced with all the durability which this art possesses. Unfortunately, however, many Daguerreotypes cannot be copied as well by the Ambrotype process, in consequence of the dark background generally adopted, the Ambrotype requiring a white background in order to copy successfully. This difficulty can be overcome in a great degree, and the Ambrotype copy produced with a light background, having all the beautiful effects so much desired in this art.

The original Daguerreotype must be first copied in the usual manner, with the black background apparent, of course, then dried, and the figure only blackened over on the reverse side, when a white piece of paper or pasteboard must be placed behind the glass, and a second copy taken with the white background apparent. The second copy will of course be taken, possessing all requisites of a good Ambrotype.

Many Daguerreotypes can be improved by this process, especially in the appearance of the background. The necessity of a double copy is required to produce the Ambrotype effect, or the first copy may be sealed with only the white paper inserted for a background. Yet the effect is not so pleasing, nor is it so durable.

COPYING ENGRAVINGS, STATUARY, MACHINERY, ETC.

Copying engravings is a very simple process, as the surface is always even, and the objects easily arranged in a favorable light. A small opening diaphragm can be used, which will render the copy very distinct in its details, actually beautifying the engraving itself.

In copying statuary, it will be necessary to have a darker background than the plain white one so often used; yet it need not be entirely black—a dark blue or brown color will answer. One having a lighter centre, and darkened at the sides, would produce a pleasing effect.

In copying models of machinery, this process is of an incalculable utility, as it can be readily seen. The exact counterpart can be produced with a perfect perspective, and no reversal of the object copied.

CHAPTER XV.

ON THE MANNER OF ARRANGING THE LIGHT—THE FALLING OF THE SAME ON THE DRAPERY—USE OF A DIAPHRAGM—LIGHT ON THE EYES—USING SCREENS—BACKGROUNDS—REFLECTORS—DIAPHRAGM—TIME IN THE CAMERA—OVER-EXPOSURE, AND UNDER-DEVELOPING—TAKING CHILDREN'S PORTRAITS.

THE proper adjustment of light for Ambrotypes is a subject which demands the utmost care, and is one which is of great importance to good success in photography. It has been found, of course, that a skylight is much more to be preferred than any side-light, although a very high side-light will answer for the purpose. A skylight that is not more than ten or fifteen feet from the sitter in the highest point, and falling over in such a manner that the lowest portion of it shall be five feet from the floor, has been found to work well. It is absolutely requisite that there should be a good volume of light on the drapery. This must be seen in the camera, for unless this is attained, the drapery will appear undefined.

By using a diaphragm with a small opening, the light becomes rather more diffused—hence the middle tints and the gradations of light and shade are more clearly seen, as well as a more perfect outline and sharpness. In consequence of the great sensitiveness in Ambrotyping, a diaphragm can be used more frequently than in the Daguerreotype process. Of course in a weak light it cannot be adopted, neither can it be used when children are the subjects.

ON SCREENS AND BACKGROUNDS.

There are three colored screens needed in an ordinary skylight—viz., blue, white, and black—the blue to be used, in connection with the white, at the side of the face, to modify the intense white that may sometimes fall on the eye; the black screen to be placed between the sitter, and at a considerable distance from him and the lower portion of the skylight, to cut off the large light that sometimes falls on the eyes.

This light on the eyes is a very important feature in producing good pictures, and it is one which is often neglected. Without a round, distinct light falling upon each eye, resembling a small *pin-head*, there can be no perfect picture produced. It will therefore be necessary to so alter and arrange the screens, and the position of the sitter, as to fulfil all these conditions before the impression is given.

The background for Ambrotypes which has come into general use is the white one, because the effect is found to be more pleasing when finished up with the black varnish. The intense white is not so apparent after the picture is finished. It assumes a much darker hue, resembling more nearly the neutral tint of the artist. If the film of the collodion is thin, the background will appear still darker.

The background should be made of strong cotton cloth, stretched on a frame of a size sufficient to be taken in the camera, without showing either side when taking groups.

An improvement can easily be made by coloring or whitewashing it with pure whiting mixed with water, in which a small quantity of glue has been dissolved. Two coats of this whitewash will render it a perfectly dead surface, which is better adapted for the purpose than plain cotton cloth, although many operators use only the white cotton cloth well bleached. As much distance as possible behind the sitter is recommended; even five or six feet, when it can be attained, will produce the best effects.

Other backgrounds than white are frequently employed. Blue, brown, and a light yellow produce very excellent impressions, if a good distance is obtained, and a strong light falls on it at the same time.

The light being well adjusted, and a good *focus* obtained as well as position, the time necessary for the exposure of the plate will of course vary according to the many conditions under which it is taken. The time will be entirely a matter of experiment, but it has been found by all successful ambrotypers that an over-exposure in the camera, combined with a short time in developing, will produce the most satisfactory results. The pictures will assume a much more desirable tone. The drapery will be well defined, and the general effect much improved by pursuing this course. It is only when children are to be taken that operators can develop slowly. The rule to be observed in children's portraits is, to sit as long as they will without moving, then develop until the picture appears. The tone is never so desirable but the likeness will be there, which is often prized by the parents more than the most splendid productions of the artist.

In developing, it may sometimes become necessary to arrest the process on the face, allowing it to continue on the drapery. This can be effected by pouring the water slowly on the face, and gradually extending it over the whole picture. Very frequently beautiful effects can be produced by this means of manipulating.

CHAPTER XVI.

ALCOHOLIC SOLUTIONS FOR PREPARING COLLODION—IODIDE OF SILVER SOLUTION—BROMIDE OF SILVER SOLUTION—BROMO-IODIDE OF SILVER SOLUTION—SATURATED SOLUTION OF IODIDE OF POTASSIUM IN ALCOHOL—OF BROMIDE OF POTASSIUM—TO MAKE HYDRO-BROMIC ACID.

The references made in a former portion of this work to the manufacture of collodion will now be given.

All the recipes here presented are highly recommended. All these collodions will work, and work well, if the proper nitrate baths are used in connection with them. But it may be found that many of them will fail at the first trial, yet if a different modification of the bath is adopted, they will work successfully.

The general rule laid down by the most experienced photographers is, that if a collodion is heavily iodized, it will require a larger quantity of silver in the nitrate bath, and, *vice versa*, a lightly iodized collodion will work with a bath of a less quantity of silver.

The formula given in the chapter on manipulating, page 180, is one which is said to be used by Rehn, of Philadelphia. It certainly will produce very pleasing effects, and if care is had in compounding, it cannot fail of absolute success.

The preparation of all collodions, however, is unavoidably attended with diverse results, from the great liability of some one of the ingredients being of an inferior quality. Nor can one be fully assured of success until the collodion is made and allowed to settle two or three days, and a trial had of the same.

This will necessarily consume much time, and also cause disappointment. It is therefore suggested that, when convenient, the collodion which has already been tested by an experienced operator and maker should be used.

Here follow the various recipes for collodions, and the baths which are necessary to accompany them.

Rehn's celebrated Recipe for Ambrotype Collodion.

No. 1. Collodion . . . . . 8 ounces.
       Iodide of silver . . . . 4 drachms.
       Hydro-bromic acid . . . 20 drops.

COLLODION RECIPES.

This collodion requires 40 grains of nitrate of silver to the ounce, with the usual developer.

No. 2.
- Collodion . . . . . 8 ounces.
- Bromo-iodide of silver . . 6 drachms.
- Hydro-bromic acid . . . 25 drops

Bath of 40 grains to the ounce.

Cutting's celebrated Patent Recipe for Ambrotype Collodion.

No. 3.
- Collodion . . . . . 1 ounce.
- Gum camphor . . . . 1 grain.
- Iodide of potassium . . . 5 grains.

30-grain nitrate bath.

No. 4.
- Collodion . . . . . 6 ounces.
- Iodide of potassium . . . 25 grains.
- Iodide of silver solution . . 2 drachms
- Iodide of ammonia . . . 5 grains.
- Iodine, pure . . . . 1 grain.

30-grain nitrate bath.

No. 5.
- Collodion . . . . . 17 ounces.
- Iodide of potassium . . . 40 grains.
- Bromide of potassium . . 40 grains.

Nitrate bath 30 grains to the ounce of water.

No. 6.
- Collodion . . . . . 4 ounces.
- Iodide of potassium . . . 12 grains.
- Bromide of potassium . . 15 grains.
- Saturated solution of iodide of potassium in alcohol } 20 drops.

Nitrate bath of 30 grains.

No. 7. Collodion . . . . . 6 ounces.
Iodide of silver solution . . 1 drachm.
Hydro-bromic acid . . . 18 drops.
Bromide of potassium . . . 5 grains.
Iodide of potassium . . . 15 grains.
Saturated solution of iodide of potassium in alcohol } $2\frac{1}{2}$ drachms.

40 grains in the nitrate bath.

Very sensitive Collodion for Children.

No. 8. Collodion . . . . . 8 ounces.
Iodide of ammonia . . . 40 grains.
Bromide of ammonia . . . 16 grains.

40 or 50 grain bath.

ALCOHOLIC SOLUTIONS FOR PREPARING COLLODION.

These solutions are to be prepared and allowed to remain several hours before using, and kept excluded from the light. When they are added to the collodion, they must always be perfectly clear and transparent, nor must any portion of the precipitate which is seen at the bottom of the preparation fall into the collodion.

It is recommended to prepare all these solutions some days even before they are needed, in order that the alcohol and potassium shall dissolve a greater proportion of the iodides or bromides of silver. The greater the proportion of silver taken up, the better chemical effect will be produced in the collodion. These various preparations are the most difficult portion to be made in manufacturing the collodion, and require the greatest care and attention.

IODIDE OF SILVER SOLUTION.

Dissolve 80 grains of iodide of potassium in 4 ounces of water, and 120 grains of nitrate of silver in the same quantity, but in a separate bottle. (This process must not be conducted in a strong daylight, but in one greatly subdued, or in a dark room by the light of a lamp.) Then pour them together in a large graduated dish, or an open glass vessel, when a yellow precipitate will be formed. This is pure iodide of silver. Wash this precipitate with water three times, allowing it to settle a few minutes, and decant or pour the water off. Then wash it with alcohol twice, to displace the water, pouring it off, and leaving the iodide of silver in the dish. This must now be placed in a glass-stoppered bottle that will hold ten or twelve ounces. Dissolve the iodide of silver in eight ounces of alcohol, 80 per cent., in which has been saturated one ounce of iodide of potassium, as follows:

Pulverize the ounce of iodide of potassium in a clean porcelain mortar, and add one or two ounces of alcohol from the eight ounces which is to be measured out for the iodide of silver solvent. Stir with a pestle the alcohol in the potassium, and a small portion will be taken up or dissolved. This must now be poured into the bottle which contains the washed iodide of silver. Then proceed in the same manner, adding two ounces more of the alcohol, stirring it well, and pouring into the bottle as much as will dissolve, until the whole eight ounces are added. There may be a portion of the iodide of potassium in the mortar not dissolved; this can also be added to the iodide of silver. After shaking it, allow it to stand and settle perfectly clear, when it will be ready for use.

BROMIDE OF SILVER SOLUTION.

Bromide of potassium	80 grains.
Nitrate of silver	80 grains.

Dissolve separately in four ounces of water; then mix it, when the bromide of silver is formed, and is seen in a precipitate at the bottom of the dish. Wash this precipitate with water three times, allowing it to settle a few minutes, and decant or pour the water off. Then wash it with alcohol twice, to displace the water, pouring it off, leaving the bromide of silver in the dish. This must now be placed in a glass-stoppered bottle that will hold ten or twelve ounces. Dissolve the bromide of silver in eight ounces of alcohol, 80 per cent., in which has been saturated one ounce of bromide of potassium.

Pulverize the ounce of bromide of potassium in a clean porcelain mortar, and add one or two ounces of alcohol from the eight ounces which are to be measured out for the bromide of silver solvent. With the pestle stir the alcohol in the potassium, and a small portion will be taken up or dissolved. This must now be poured into the bottle which contains the washed bromide of silver. Then proceed in the same manner, adding two ounces more of the alcohol, stirring it well, and pouring into the bottle as much as will dissolve, until the whole eight ounces are added.

BROMO-IODIDE OF SILVER SOLUTION.

Dissolve separately in four ounces of water—

Bromide of potassium	80 grains.
Nitrate of silver	80 grains.

Then mix and wash out with water three times, and with alcohol twice. Then pulverize one ounce of iodide of potassium, and dissolve in eight ounces of alcohol, precisely in the same manner as described in the alcoholic solution of iodide of silver.

These various solutions of silver, and iodides and bromides, are deemed very essential to success in ambrotyping. If they are prepared with care and attention, none can fail of success in making good collodion.

They should be kept as much from the light as possible, and always in glass-stoppered bottles well filled, to prevent evaporation.

SATURATED SOLUTION OF IODIDE OF POTASSIUM IN ALCOHOL.

Pulverize one ounce of iodide of potassium in a mortar, and add three ounces of 80 per cent. alcohol, stirring it for some minutes, and then allowing it to settle. Pour off the clear liquid into a bottle, and add a smaller quantity of alcohol, stirring this also in the same manner, and pouring off the clear solution into the bottle. Continue to add each time a smaller quantity of alcohol, until all the potassium is dissolved.

SATURATED SOLUTION OF BROMIDE OF POTASSIUM IN ALCOHOL.

Pulverize one ounce of bromide of potassium in a mortar, as described in the preparation of iodide of potassium above, adding alcohol, 80 per cent., in the same manner, until it is all dissolved.

These saturated solutions will be found very useful to add to collodions that will not work well, or if the film is not of sufficient thickness on withdrawal from the bath. By adding a small quantity of each of these saturated solutions, any desired effect can be produced.

They also enter in the properties of some of the collodion recipes given in this work.

The quantity of each saturated solution used, is for bromide of potassium just one half as much as of the iodide of potassium—that is to say, if one drachm of iodide is used, one half drachm of the bromide would be sufficient.

TO MAKE THE HYDRO-BROMIC ACID.

Alcohol (95 per cent.)	4 ounces.
Water (distilled)	1 ounce.

To this is added one drachm of pure bromine,— then shaken quickly, and allowed to remain for twenty-four hours. It will assume at first a deep cherry-red color, but afterwards it will become clear again. Every twenty-four hours there must be added, say, five or six drops more of bromine, and continued for a week or ten days, adding a few drops every day, when it will be ready for use. It will eventually assume nearly a white transparent color, slightly inclined to yellow.

This preparation is highly sensitive to light, and must be kept in a perfectly air-tight bottle, and not exposed to the light of day.

CHAPTER XVII.

PREPARATION OF THE VARNISHES—WHITE COPAL VARNISH—GUM-DEMAR VARNISH—BLACK ASPHALTUM VARNISH—WHITE VARNISH OF SHELLAC AND COPAL—THICKENED VARNISH FOR CEMENTING GLASSES, IN PLACE OF CANADA BALSAM—GUM-SHELLAC VARNISH FOR PLATE-HOLDERS—APPLYING THE VARNISHES.

These varnishes for Ambrotypes are somewhat difficult to prepare, and likely to soil the hands in their manufacture. It is well, therefore, to purchase them ready for use, thereby saving much trouble. However, a few recipes will be given for those who wish to manufacture their own.

WHITE COPAL.

Select the whitest portions of white copal gum, and dissolve, say, one ounce in two ounces of turpentine. The copal is first to be pulverized, and added to the turpentine, and allowed to dissolve. If the varnish is too thick for use, add more turpentine.

GUM-DEMAR VARNISH.

Gum-demar	½ ounce.
Chloroform	2 ounces.

These must be allowed to stand after shaking for two or three days, until the gum is all dissolved, then decanted off into a separate bottle, avoiding the sediment at the bottom.

This varnish is highly recommended for using on collodion pictures that have been colored. By pouring this carefully over, it will not disturb the color, and it dries readily, nor is it so liable to change by the action of light.

BLACK ASPHALTUM VARNISH.

Asphaltum, pulverized	1 ounce.

Adding spirits of turpentine, and stirring it well in a mortar, until all is dissolved. Any consistency can be had which is desired, by adding more or less of the turpentine. A portion of the asphaltum may not dissolve; this can be left in the bottom of the mortar, and rejected entirely.

WHITE VARNISH OF SHELLAC AND COPAL.

Alcohol, 95 per cent.

New Zealand gum	1 ounce.
Gum-shellac	½ ounce.
Gum-copal	¼ ounce.

Add sufficient alcohol to these three gums to dissolve them in a mortar, and a transparent varnish is obtained, of superior quality.

THICK WHITE VARNISHES FOR CEMENTING GLASSES WITHOUT THE USE OF CANADA BALSAM.

Gum-copal pulverized in a mortar, adding spirits of turpentine gradually, but only enough to dissolve it to form a consistency of Venice turpentine, or balsam of fir, produces the finest effect on the application of the two glasses.

GUM-SHELLAC VARNISH FOR PLATE-HOLDERS.

Dissolve sufficient of gum-shellac in 95 per cent. alcohol to render it the consistency of cream.

This varnish should be always on hand ready for use, to varnish over the photographic frames or plate-holders, as the action of the acid in the bath will cause the glasses in the corner to become loosened. By applying this simple varnish with a brush, the glasses will remain in their places, and prevent the action of the nitrate of silver. The proper time to apply this varnish is in the afternoon, after the plate-holders are laid aside, because it will require some time for them to dry.

Before applying the varnish, be careful to remove all moisture from the holders, and varnish all that portion of the plate-holders that is subject to being wetted by the solution of the nitrate bath.

APPLYING THE VARNISHES.

The white varnishes are always applied in the same manner as the collodion—viz., by pouring it on the surface, and allowing it to run off at one corner into the bottle. It is necessary in applying most white varnishes that the glass plate should be slightly warmed, either by the fire or spirit-lamp, avoiding all dust or moisture. To entirely remove the dirty particles, it will be proper to filter the varnish through a thin white linen or cotton cloth.

The black varnish can be applied in the same manner. It may be dried very quickly by placing it near a gentle heat, or laying it in the sun. Of course it must be laid in a perfectly horizontal position.

A soft camel's-hair brush may be used to apply the black varnish; and if it is applied thin, it will dry in much less time. A second application of the varnish can be made, should the first not prove intense enough.

For protection, it is well to place a piece of

pasteboard (which has been previously blackened with the black varnish and dried) on the back of the glass, with the blackened side towards the varnish. This insures a perfect black on the collodion, even if the varnish is very thin; and if held by transmitted light, it would have a brownish appearance. It likewise affords a protection to the glass, avoiding breakage in case the picture falls to the ground.

Some operators have adopted the black-glazed paper. This presents too high polish for good effects, and will sometimes be seen through the varnish. A perfectly deadened surface of black is required to produce the effect. Black cotton velvet answers the purpose, and, as will be seen, has been adopted in all the transparent cases used for Ambrotypes. Cases lined with black velvet are being adopted for these pictures.

CHAPTER XVIII.

CAUSES OF FAILURE IN THE PRACTICE OF THE ART—FOGGING THE PICTURES—TO DETECT THE FOGGING OF PLATES—BLACK AND WHITE SPECKS ON THE PLATES—TRANSPARENT AND OPAQUE SPOTS—IMPURITY OF CHEMICALS—SPOTS OR STREAKS ON THE GLASS PLATES.

The process is so full of variations in the details of practice, and the chemicals are so liable to be affected by the slightest change, that many who are induced to adopt this art meet with difficulties in great abundance.

Failures in the art were formerly considered a general rule, and a matter of certainty, while good pictures were regarded as fortunate exceptions. We have, however, progressed so far, that this state of things has not been encountered in the practice of late years, and we are now enabled to proceed with some degree of certainty.

Nevertheless, the art is not yet perfect, and

failures will meet the early practitioner at the threshold of his profession, and perhaps intimidate his too confident expectations of success.

The various causes of failures will be explained in as clear and lucid a manner as possible; yet there may be some causes overlooked which may occur to others that have not been observed. We are indebted to Mr. Hardwich, of London, for much information on this subject, and it is hoped the author will not be deemed presumptuous if he profits by the experience of that ablest of photographers of the present day.

FOGGING THE PICTURE.

The "fogging," as it is termed, will most frequently occur from a too careless *exclusion of light*. The liability to this failure is obvious, for the slightest trace of white daylight falling upon the plate will surely cause fogging. It will therefore be highly important to guard against this oft recurring obstacle.

Fogging is sometimes attributable to weak collodion, or to a bath too weak, and sometimes to over-developing. In order to detect the ultimate cause of this failure, when it occurs, a series of experiments may be made as follows:

PLAN OF PROCEEDING IN ORDER TO DETECT THE CAUSE OF THE FOGGING.

If the operator has had but little experience in the collodion process, and is using good Ambrotype collodion of great sensitiveness in a new bath, the probability is that the cause of fogging will be *over-exposure.* Having obviated this, which can easily be done by shortening the time, proceed to test the bath, and add sufficient acetic or nitric acid to give a faint acid reaction to testpaper.

Next prepare a plate as usual, and immediately on its removal from the bath, pour on the developer: after a few seconds wash, fix, and bring it out to the light. If any mistiness is perceptible, *the developing room is in fault.*

On the other hand, if the plate remains absolutely clear under these circumstances, *it is possible that the cause of error may be in the camera.* Prepare another plate, place it in the camera, and proceed exactly as if taking a picture, neglecting, however, to expose the plate to the action of light. Allow it to remain for two or three minutes, and then remove and develop as usual.

If no indication of the cause of fogging be

obtained by either of these ways, there is every reason to suppose that it is due to *diffused light* gaining entrance through the lenses, or some portion of the camera box.

BLACK AND WHITE SPECKS UPON THE PLATE.

Opaque or transparent dots, thickly studding every part of the plate, are produced by the following causes:

1. *The use of collodion containing floating particles.*—Each particle becomes a centre of chemical action, and produces a speck or black spot.

Collodion should never be employed immediately after mixing, but placed aside to settle for several hours, after which the upper portion may be poured off for use. This is especially necessary when the double iodide of potassium and silver is employed: the salt is decomposed to a certain extent by *dilution*, and small particles of iodide of silver separate, which eventually settle to the bottom of the bottle.

2. *Dust upon the surface of the glass at the time of pouring on the collodion.*—Thoroughly cleaned glasses, if set aside for a few minutes, accumulate small particles of dust. Each plate, therefore, should be gently wiped with a silk handkerchief,

or a buckskin buff made in the form of a ball, immediately before being used, and lastly dusted with a camel's-hair brush.

3. *Where an inferior kind of glass is used.*— The surface of an inferior quality of glass is oftentimes roughed and studded with minute specks. Occasionally these can be removed by means of diluted acid.

TRANSPARENT AND OPAQUE SPOTS.

Spots are of two kinds—spots of *opacity*, which appear *black* when seen by transmitted light, and *white* by reflected light, and spots of *transparency*, the reverse of the others, being white when seen on negatives, and black on positives.

Opaque spots are referable to *an excess of development* at the point where the spot is seen. They may be caused by—

1. *The nitrate solution being turbid*, or from flakes of iodide of silver having fallen away into the solution by use of an over-iodized collodion; from a deposit formed by degrees upon the sides of the gutta percha trough; from the inside of the trough being *dusty* at the time of pouring in the solution. In order to obviate these inconveniences, it is well to make at least half as much again of

the nitrate solution as is necessary, and to keep it in the large bottle, from which the upper part may be poured off as it is required.

2. *Faults in the plate-holder.*—Sometimes a small hole exists in the slide, which admits a pencil of light, and produces a spot known by its being always in the same place. Occasionally the door works too tightly, so that small particles of wood, &c., are scraped off and projected against the plate when it is raised; or perhaps the operator, after the exposure is finished, shuts down the slide too quickly, and causes a splash in the liquid, which has drained down and accumulated in the groove below. This cause, although not a common one, may sometimes occur.

Spots of transparency are produced in a manner altogether different from that of the others.

1. They may generally be traced to some cause *which renders the iodide of silver insensitive to light at that particular point,* so that on the application of the developer no reduction takes place.

2. *Concentration of the nitrate of silver on the surface of the film by evaporation.*—When the film becomes too dry after removal from the bath, the solvent power of the nitrate increases so much that it is apt to eat away the iodide, and produce spots.

3. *By raising the plate off the nitrate bath too quickly after its first immersion.*

4. *By pouring on the developer entirely on one portion of the plate*, by which the nitrate of silver is washed away, and the development prevented.

5. *By use of glasses improperly cleaned.*—This cause is perhaps the most frequent of all. Great care should therefore be observed in cleaning the glasses, and in keeping them in good order, and in readiness for the collodion.

IMPURITY OF CHEMICALS, ETC.

Chemicals are so liable to be of inferior quality, that this cause of failure is indeed one that appears almost insurmountable; yet, although a great difficulty here presents itself, there is a possibility of obtaining good material, and they should be sought till they are found.

The vapors of ammonia or bromine, or even iodine, will cause the plate to become covered with spots or stains.

SPOTS OR STREAKS, ETC.

Spots or streaks which are yet black, coming from the corner where the plate is held by the fingers, are caused by hyposulphite or cyanide of potassium in some manner running from the hand. Streaks that are parallel, running up and down the plate, are caused by the dust floating in the bath at the time of immersion.

Streaks which lie in the bed of the collodion, looking like rivers laid down on a map, are caused by not washing the plate sufficiently after the developing solution has been applied.

Streaks or lines resembling muslin, and streaks which have a cloudy appearance, occur when the collodion is thicker on some portion of the plate than on another. The streaks resembling leaves are also due to the same cause. If there is not a sufficient quantity of acetic acid in the developer, it will not flow evenly over the plate, and will invariably cause streaks.

CHAPTER XIX.

CAUTIONS WITH REGARD TO USING THE VARIOUS CHEMICAL SUBSTANCES IN MAKING GUN-COTTON—USE OF ETHER AND ALCOHOL—USE OF CYANIDE OF POTASSIUM—NITRATE OF SILVER—CLEANING THE HANDS—SOLUTION FOR CLEANING THE HANDS—HINTS ON THE VARIOUS PROCESSES CONNECTED WITH POSITIVES AND NEGATIVES—TO RENDER COLLODION HIGHLY SENSITIVE—THE LAMPRATYPE PROCESS.

In the practice of the photographic art, great caution is necessary to be observed in regard to the various chemicals employed.

By a singular coincidence of circumstances, very many of the chemicals are combustible, and are indeed of a very explosive nature, while those which are not inflammable are poisonous. It will therefore be the wish of every operator to avoid accidents, as they are always liable to occur unless they are carefully guarded against.

In preparing gun-cotton, the vapors arising from the combination of the acid and nitrate of potash are very deleterious, if inhaled, as they are liable to be, because it is necessary to stir the cotton during the whole time of immersion. Always prepare it in the open air, or where a free circulation of it may be obtained.

When the cotton is drying, avoid any contact of fire, or an approach to the fire, for it explodes at the temperature of 370° Fahrenheit, while gunpowder requires 500°. If gun-cotton is kept a long time in large quantities, spontaneous combustion may ensue, if any moisture comes in contact with it.

In using ether and alcohol, be careful to remove the lamp to a great distance from it. In pouring the collodion on the plate, one is very liable to accident, for the vapors of ether are rapidly passing off. They will ignite even if the lamp is within one or two feet of the bottle. Coat the plates by the light of day, if possible, thereby avoiding the possibility of combustion of the collodion.

In pouring ether or collodion from one bottle to another, practice the greatest care, as the vapors will ignite at a long distance from these substances, when they are made to evaporate.

Cyanide of potassium will have the effect of a virulent poison, if taken in the system; and even inhaling the fumes which constantly arise from it are injurious. By wetting the lips slightly with alcohol immediately afterwards, it will in some degree neutralize the unpleasant effects.

Use no soap to remove the stains of nitrate of silver, but employ cyanide of potassium, which must be well washed with clean water to remove any traces of that substance. Should the skin be broken, a small quantity of cyanide will enter, causing considerable pain and inconvenience.

Avoid the contact of the hands as much as possible with the nitrate of silver solution, as well as dropping it upon the clothes. Wherever it may fall, it will cause a stain or mark that nothing but cyanide of potassium will remove.

TO CLEAN THE HANDS.

The most effectual way to clean the fingers when they become stained with nitrate of silver, is to moisten them and rub them with cyanide of potassium. This should be used as soon as possible after the stains have been made.

A piece of pumice-stone rubbed down to a flat surface is also very effectual in removing fresh stains.

ANOTHER PLAN.

Wash the hands with a solution of iodine, dissolved in alcohol, and while they are wet wash with a strong solution of hyposulphite of soda, afterwards with water, to remove all traces of the salt.

METHOD OF REMOVING THE STAINS OF SILVER FROM LINEN, THE HANDS, ETC.

Mix together—

Common alcohol	20 parts.
Iodine	1 part.
Nitric acid	1 part.
Hydrochloric acid	1 part.

These produce a reddish liquid, which, when applied to stains caused by any salts of silver, immediately converts them into chloride and iodide of silver, soluble in hyposulphite of soda and cyanide of potassium. The effect is especially marked on stained linen. When a black patch is touched with the liquid, by means of a little brush, it instantly turns yellow, with a violet border, if the linen has been starched. On washing with the hyposulphite, or with the cyanide, the violet tint immediately vanishes, and the yellow spot by degrees. It is well to wash the stained place after the application of the iodized solution, in order to remove the acids, which might produce independent stains by contact with the hyposulphite or the cyanide.

For the hands, the operation is the same, except that, instead of using a brush, the skin may be rubbed with a piece of rag or cotton.

HINTS AND SUGGESTIONS.

The following hints and suggestions in regard to the practice may be observed with profit:

Always keep the stoppers in the bottle, except when the bottle is in actual use.

Always cover the nitrate of silver bath, except when in use.

Always rinse the fingers well in clean water after developing a picture, or the next will probably be injured.

The frames for holding the glass plates in the plate-holder will require revarnishing, as the nitrate of silver often acts on the wood, and produces stains on the picture.

Frequently wash the glass bottles containing the developing solution.

Be careful that the towels and clothes for cleaning the glasses are used for no other purpose, and are free from all contact of soap, &c.

Remove carefully any dried collodion which may form about the neck of the bottle.

Particularly observe that in every thing connected with photography, the most scrupulous attention to cleanliness is indispensable to good success.

Remember to decant from the large bottle a sufficient quantity of collodion every evening for use the following day into several small bottles, as the oftener it is decanted, the more pure the collodion.

If the collodion is too thick, and requires the addition of more ether, the proper time to add it will be when it is decanted. It may then be slightly agitated.

Avoid in all cases the shaking of collodion, or of the varnishes. The collodion is always throwing down a precipitate which requires many hours to fall again, if disturbed; and the varnish will become full of air-bubbles, which on being applied to the surface of the plate, greatly injure it.

In applying the thick varnish, or the balsam, between the two glasses, according to the "patent process," great care must be observed to avoid the air-bubbles. It should be poured only on the centre of the glass, and then with only a drop or two. After the pouring, the balsam should form a slight line, running to the edge of the glass, otherwise air-bubbles will inevitably be produced. Avoid pressing the glasses after they are sealed.

Use gutta-percha dishes for all photographic purposes, and avoid bringing them too near the fire, as they will melt at a low temperature.

In using test-papers, observe the following precautions: They should be kept in a dark place, and protected from the action of the air, or they soon become purple from carbonic acid, always present in the atmosphere in small quantities. By immersion in water containing about one drop of liquor potasse in four ounces, the blue color is restored.

Test-papers prepared with *porous* paper show the red color better than those upon glazed or strongly sized paper. If the quantity of acid present, however, is small, it is not sufficient in any case simply to dip the paper in the liquid: a small strip should be thrown in, and allowed to remain for ten minutes or a quarter of an hour.

If the paper, on immersion, assumes a wine-red, or purple tint, in place of a decided red, it is probably caused by carbonic acid gas. In that case the blue color returns when the paper is washed and held to the fire. Blue litmus-paper may be changed to the red papers used for alkalies by soaking in water acidified with sulphuric acid, one drop to half a pint.

TO RENDER ANY COLLODION HIGHLY SENSITIVE.

By the addition of two or three drops of a solution of iodide of iron in alcohol to every ounce of iodized collodion, it will cause it to make the impression in the camera in an incredible short space of time; but as it soon injures the quality of the collodion, it is well not to sensitize only as much as is wanted for immediate use.

TO DARKEN AMBROTYPES,

OR THE LAMPRATYPE.

A new and ingenious plan has been devised and successfully carried into practice by Mr. S. A. Holmes, of New York, of rendering Ambrotypes much darker in the dark portions of the picture, and whiter in the white portions. For distinction, he has named them Lampratypes.

The method of effecting this is as follows:

THE LAMPRATYPE PROCESS.

After the picture is well dried on the glass, and before applying any varnish, gently rub it, on the collodion side, with a round buckskin buff ball, made of the softest quality of buckskin, and tied very lightly over cotton. This buff must be used for no other purpose. Pass the buff lightly across the plate in straight lines, and it will assume a darker hue until the desired shade is attained.

By this same process a portion of the hair that may be too light, can be rendered darker by rubbing it lightly with a brush, or camel's-hair pencil; or any portion of the drapery may be changed to a darker shade, if desirable.

TO MAKE THE PEARL AMBROTYPES.

Dissolve one ounce of bi-chloride of mercury (corrosive sublimate) in half an ounce of pure muriatic acid, and add to this six ounces of water; or a saturated solution of bi-chloride in water will answer as well. As soon as the ambrotype is finished in the usual manner, and ready for drying, place it on a Daguerreotype gilding-stand, and pour sufficient of this solution over the plate to cover it, allowing it to remain for a few minutes. At first it will assume a dark color, and lines appear on its surface; but if allowed to remain a short time, or if a small degree of heat from a spirit-lamp is applied, it will soon change to a beautiful clear pearl white, the lights and shades being very transparent.

When the requisite color is attained, great care must be used in washing the solution from the plate, as the collodion is affected by the acid.

These pictures can only be slightly colored, and only the white varnish applied, and backed with a blackened glass, without any transparent medium.

The black varnish cannot be applied to the collodion side, in consequence of the great transparency.

Impressions which are too short time in the camera, may be rendered white and sufficiently clear by this process—hence it is very useful for taking children's portraits, and has been adopted by many with great success.

CHAPTER XX.

VOCABULARY OF PHOTOGRAPHIC CHEMICALS—ACETIC ACID—ALCOHOL—AMMONIA—BROMINE—BROMIDE OF POTASSIUM—CARBONATE OF SODA—CYANIDE OF POTASSIUM—CHLORIDE OF GOLD—HYPOSULPHITE OF GOLD—HYPOSULPHITE OF SODA—IODINE—IODIDE OF AMMONIA—IODIDE OF POTASSIUM—IODIDE OF SILVER—PROTOSULPHATE OF IRON—LITMUS—NITRIC ACID—NITRATE OF POTASH—NITRATE OF SILVER—SULPHURIC ACID—PROPERTIES OF ETHER—PROPERTIES OF WATER.

A VOCABULARY of the principal chemicals used in the photographic art is deemed necessary mainly for purposes of reference. It frequently may occur to the experienced operator, that a more intimate knowledge of the construction of the ingredients used in the art is required, and this can be supplied in a good measure without a reference to large works on chemistry.

This vocabulary is not to be considered as a complete one on the subject; but only so far as one may require information specially connected with the practice of this art, will this be found useful.

The symbols are omitted, for the reason that, if used, they would require further explanation, and continue to lead the more inexperienced chemist into difficulties, and would render the book too prolix with chemical terms. Some of these terms, however, are unavoidably introduced.

ACETIC ACID.

Acetic acid is a product of the *oxidation* of alcohol. Spirituous liquids, when perfectly pure, are not affected by exposure to air; but if a portion of yeast, or *nitrogenous organic matter* of any kind is added, it soon acts as a *ferment*, and causes the spirit to unite with oxygen derived from the atmosphere, and so to become *sour* from formation of vinegar, or acetic acid, as it is properly termed.

The most concentrated acetic acid is obtained by neutralizing common vinegar with carbonate of soda, and crystallizing out the acetate of soda so formed; this acetate of soda is then distilled with sulphuric acid, which removes the soda and liberates acetic acid: the acetic acid being volatile, distils over, and may be condensed.

Properties of Acetic Acid.—The strongest acid contains only a single atom of water; it is sold under the name of "*glacial acetic acid,*" so called from its property of solidifying at a moderately low temperature. At about fifty degrees the crystals melt, and form a limpid liquid of pungent odor, and a density nearly corresponding to that of water. The specific gravity of acetic acid, however, is no test of its real strength, which can only be estimated by analysis.

In purchasing the commercial acid (which is generally known as Acetic Acid No. 8) for photographic purposes, it is important to distinguish the *glacial acid* from a liquid of "*ten per cent. real acid*" sometimes sold; also it is well to test for the presence of *sulphuric acid*, which may be recognized by the white precipitate produced on adding a drop of solution of chloride of barium.

ALCOHOL.

Alcohol is obtained by the careful distillation of any spirituous or fermented liquor. If wine or beer be placed in a retort, and heat applied, the alcohol, being more volatile than water, rises first, and is condensed in an appropriate receiver; a portion of the vapor of water, however, passes over with the alcohol, and dilutes it to a certain degree, forming what is termed "spirits of wine." In order to render the alcohol thoroughly *anhydrous*, it is necessary to employ the *quick-lime*, which possesses a still greater attraction for water. An equal weight of this powdered lime is mixed with the alcohol, and the two are distilled together.

Properties of Alcohol.—Pure anhydrous alcohol is a limpid liquid, of an agreeable odor and pungent taste; specific gravity at 60·794. It absorbs vapor of water, and becomes diluted by exposure to damp air; boils at 1.73 Fahrenheit. It has never been frozen.

Alcohol distilled from carbonate of potash, has a specific gravity of ·823, and contains 90 per cent. of real spirit.

The specific gravity of ordinary rectified spirits of wine is usually about .840, and it contains 80 to 83 per cent. of absolute alcohol.

AMMONIA.

The liquid known by this name is an aqueous solution of a volatile gas.

Ammoniacal gas contains one atom of nitrogen combined with three of hydrogen. These elementary bodies exhibit no affinity for each other, but they can be made to unite under certain circumstances, and the result is ammonia.

Properties of Ammonia.—Ammoniacal gas is soluble in water to a large extent; the solution possesses those properties which are termed *alkaline*. Ammonia, however, differs from the other alkalies in one important particular—it is volatile; hence the original color of turmeric paper, affected by ammonia, is restored on the application of heat. Solution of ammonia absorbs carbonic acid rapidly from the air, and is converted into carbonate of ammonia; it should therefore be preserved in stoppered bottles. Besides carbonate, commercial ammonia often contains chloride of ammonia, recognized by the white precipitate given by nitrate of silver after acidifying with pure nitric acid.

The strength of commercial ammonia varies greatly. That sold for pharmaceutical purposes, under the name of Liquor Ammoniæ, contains about ten per cent. of real ammonia.

The specific gravity of aqueous ammonia diminishes with the proportion of ammonia present, the liquor ammoniæ being usually about ·936.

BROMINE.

This elementary substance is obtained from the uncrystallizable residue of sea-water, termed *bittern*. It exists in the water in very minute proportion, and combined with magnesium, in the form of a soluble bromide.

Properties.—Bromine is a deep reddish-brown liquid of a disagreeable odor, and fuming strongly at common temperatures; sparingly soluble in water (1 part in 23—Löwig), but more abundantly so in alcohol, and especially in ether. Specific gravity 3·0.

Bromine is closely analogous to chlorine and iodine in its chemical properties. It stands on the list intermediately between the two—its affinities being stronger than those of iodine, but weaker than chlorine. It is a powerful poison.

BROMIDE OF POTASSIUM.

Bromide of potassium is prepared by adding bromine to caustic potash, and heating the product, which is a mixture of bromide of potassium and bromate of potash, to redness, in order to drive off the oxygen from the latter salt. It crystallizes in anhydrous tubes like the chloride and iodide of potassium; it is easily soluble in water, but more sparingly so in alcohol; it yields red fumes of bromine when acted upon by sulphuric acid.

CARBONATE OF SODA.

This salt was formerly obtained from the ashes of sea-weeds, but is now more economically manufactured on a large scale from common salt. The chloride of sodium is first converted into sulphate of soda, and afterwards the sulphate into carbonate of soda.

Properties.—The perfect crystals contain ten atoms of water, which are driven off by the application of heat, leaving a white powder—the anhydrous carbonate. *Common washing soda* is a neutral carbonate, contaminated to a certain extent with chloride of sodium and sulphate of soda. Carbonate of soda is soluble in twice its weight of water at 60°, the solution being strongly alkaline.

CYANIDE OF POTASSIUM.

This salt is a compound of prussic acid with potassium, and a very deadly poison. It is used in photography: added to nitrate of silver, it yields cyanide of silver, which is very sensitive to the action of light; but when added to the iodide and the fluoride of potassium, it forms a triple salt of great sensitiveness. Cyanide of silver is insoluble in water, and in diluted nitric acid. It is decomposed by hydrochloric acid, and changed into chloride of silver. Solution of ammonia, the alkaline cyanides, and especially hyposulphite of soda, dissolve it.

The cyanide of potassium dissolves the iodide, chloride, and bromide of silver; hence it is used as a fixing agent for ambrotypes. It also dissolves the protoxides and suboxides of this metal when they are precipitated by gallic acid. A solution of the salt is useful, with the aid of a brush, to remove the black spots which injure positive pictures on paper, only it must be applied with great caution, and the print immersed in water immediately after its application, else it may destroy it entirely.

CHLORIDE OF GOLD.

This salt is formed by dissolving metallic gold in nitro-hydrochloric acid, or *aqua regia*, and evaporating at a gentle heat. The solution affords deliquescent crystals of a deep orange-color.

Properties.—The solution of terchloride of gold is of a bright yellow color when dilute, but nearly red if concentrated. As usually sold, it contains an excess of hydrochloric acid; but even if freed from this, it is still acid to test-paper, although neutral, chemically speaking. It is decomposed with precipitation of metallic gold by charcoal, sulphurous acid, and many of the vegetable acids; also by protosulphate or protonitrate of iron. It tinges the cuticle of an indelible purple tint. It is soluble in alcohol, and also in ether.

The addition of *ammonia* to terchloride of gold produces the dangerous explosive compound known as *fulminating gold.*

HYPOSULPHITE OF GOLD.

Hyposulphite of gold is produced by the reaction of chloride of gold upon hyposulphite of soda.

The salt sold in commerce as *sel d'or* is a double hyposulphite of gold and soda, containing one atom of the former salt to three of the latter, with four atoms of water of crystallization.

HYPOSULPHITE OF SODA.

This salt is very soluble in water at all temperatures. It is of great service in photography for "fixing" the positive pictures on paper, which it accomplishes by dissolving the salts of silver, such as the chloride, iodide, &c., which are insoluble in water, and so removing them from the picture, and thereby preventing any further chemical change in the impression. The solution of hyposulphite of soda, after it retains some of the salts of silver in solution, is more useful for the fixing process, as it gives better black tones than when first employed. It is the best fixing material yet discovered, both for positives on paper and negatives on glass; and by careful manipulation, almost every variety of tone can be given to the pictures. With faint positive pictures, it is best to soak them for a few hours in a bath of clean water before submitting them to the action of the hyposulphite of soda, by which means the soluble salts of silver are removed without affecting those parts acted upon by the light, which constitute the blacks. Thus we abridge the time necessary for the action of the hyposulphite, and the fixed image is found to be more vigorous than if it had been placed at once in the hyposulphite of soda.

IODINE.

Iodine is chiefly prepared at Glasgow, from *kelp*, which is the fused ash obtained by burning seaweeds. The waters of the ocean contain minute quantities of the iodides of sodium and magnesium, which are separated and stored up by the growing tissues of the marine plant.

Properties.—Iodine is met with in two forms— the commercial and the resublimed iodine. The former, which is sold at a lower price than the other, is sufficiently pure for most purposes.

Iodine has a bluish black color and metallic lustre. It stains the skin yellow, and has a pungent smell, like diluted chlorine. It is extremely volatile when moist, boils at 350°, and produces dense violet-colored fumes, which condense in brilliant plates. Specific gravity 4·946. Iodine is very sparingly soluble in water, one part requiring 7,000 parts for perfect solution. Even this minute quantity, however, tinges the liquid of a brown color. Alcohol and ether dissolve it more abundantly, forming dark-brown solutions. Iodine also dissolves freely in solutions of the alkaline iodides—such as the iodide of potassium, of sodium, and of ammonium.

Chemical properties.—Iodine belongs to the chlorine group of elements, characterized by forming acids with hydrogen, and combining extensively with the metals. They are, however, comparatively indifferent to oxygen, and also to each other.

The iodides of the alkalies, and alkaline earths, are soluble in water; also those of iron, zinc, cadmium, etc. The iodides of lead, silver, and mercury are nearly or quite insoluble.

Iodine possesses the property of forming a compound of a deep-blue color with starch. In using this as a test, it is necessary, first, to liberate the iodine (if in combination) by means of chlorine, or nitric acid saturated with peroxide of nitrogen. The presence of alcohol or ether interferes to a certain extent with the result.

IODIDE OF AMMONIA.

The hydriodate of ammonia is a compound very easily decomposed: it must be kept suspended in a bottle containing a small quantity of carbonate of ammonia.

Sensitive papers may be prepared by washing them with a solution of this substance previous to placing them upon the aceto-nitrate of silver; an impression is received with great rapidity, which is developed with facility by gallic aid, to which a little acetate of ammonia has been added.

IODIDE OF POTASSIUM.

Iodide of potassium is one of the principal

chemical agents in photography. It serves to form the iodide of silver, which is the sensitive salt upon which light acts with the greatest energy. This iodide of silver is insoluble in water, but soluble in hyposulphite of soda, which is used for "*fixing*" the negative pictures.

This salt is usually formed by dissolving iodine in solution of potash until it begins to acquire a brown color; a mixture of iodide of potassium and *iodide of potash* is thus formed; but by evaporation and heating to redness, the latter salt parts with its oxygen, and is converted into iodide of potassium.

Properties.—It forms cubic and prismatic crystals, which should be very hard, and *very slightly or not at all deliquescent.* Soluble in less than an equal weight of water at 60°; it is also soluble in alcohol, but not in ether.

IODIDE OF SILVER.

Iodide of silver is obtained by adding iodide of potassium to a solution of nitrate of silver; decomposition ensues, the nitric acid leaves the silver and unites with the potash, while the liberated iodine combines with the silver, and falls as a yellow precipitate, which must be well washed in distilled water, being insoluble therein, to remove the nitrate of potash, and then dissolved in a saturated solution of iodide of potassium. This mixture is to be added to the collodion in small quantities at a time, and agitated until dissolved.

PROTOSULPHATE OF IRON.

This is the copperas or green vitriol of commerce—a most abundant substance, and used for a variety of purposes in the arts. Commercial sulphate of iron, however, being prepared on a large scale, mostly requires recrystallizing in order to render it sufficiently pure for photographic purposes.

Pure sulphate of iron is met with in the form of large, transparent, prismatic crystals, of a delicate green color; by exposure to the air they gradually absorb oxygen, and become rusty on the surface. Solution of sulphate of iron, colorless at first, afterwards changes to a red tint, and deposits a brown powder; this powder is a *basic* persulphate of iron, that is to say, a persulphate containing an excess of the oxide, or "*base*." By adding sulphuric acid to the solution of protosulphate of iron, the formation of a deposit is prevented, but the decomposition goes on slowly as before.

LITMUS.

Litmus is a vegetable substance, prepared from various *lichens*, which are principally collected on rocks adjoining the sea. The coloring matter is extracted by a peculiar process, and afterwards made up into a paste with chalk, plaster of Paris, etc.

Litmus occurs in commerce in the form of small cubes, of a fine violet color. In using it for the preparation of test-papers, it is digested in hot water, and sheets of porous paper are soaked in the blue liquid so formed. The red papers are prepared in a similar manner, and afterwards placed in water which has been rendered faintly acid with sulphuric or hydrochloric acid.

NITRIC ACID.

This acid is obtained by distilling a mixture of equal parts, by weight, of nitrate of potash and sulphuric acid. It is very abundant in commerce, and is useful in photography to form the nitrate of silver; and in combination with muriatic acid (*aqua regia*), to yield the chloride of gold: added to the sulphate of the protoxide of iron, it converts it into the sulphate of the peroxide.

It is also employed to darken the tone of the shadows of the positive paper pictures, after they have been submitted to the action of the hyposulphite of soda. Its action is similar to that of the muriatic acid used for the same purpose.

As it possesses great solvent powers, it is very useful for removing the deposits left on the gutta-percha or porcelain dishes, &c.; but the greatest care must be taken that no free acid appears in any of the preparations used in photography; for however useful in its combinations with silver, &c., alone, it has a most destructive influence by its deoxydizing qualities, neutralizing the effects produced by the agency of light.

NITRATE OF POTASH.

This salt, also termed *nitre* or *saltpetre*, is an abundant natural product, found effloresced upon the soil in certain parts of the East Indies. It is also produced artificially in what are called nitre-beds.

NITRATE OF SILVER.

Nitrate of silver is the most important ingredient in photography. It is a compound of nitric acid with the metal silver in its highest state of oxydation. It is decomposed by iodide of potassium, by which iodide of silver is obtained. The best nitrate of silver is in thin colorless crystalline plates, which are soluble in an equal weight of cold water. Exposed to light, this salt blackens, especially if any organic matter is present. Advantage is taken of this peculiar property to prepare the sensitive solutions which are spread upon the paper and glass, and other media employed in obtaining photographic pictures. It is readily decomposed by chlorides, bromides, fluorides, cyanides, &c., producing salts of exquisite sensibility; and if these, or some of them, are added to the iodide of potassium, in the first preparation of the paper, when they are submitted to the contact of the nitrate of silver, compounds are formed, apparently intermediate in their atomic constitution, between the protoxide and the suboxide of silver. As soon as the light strikes these preparations in this condition, they pass from the state intermediate between the protoxide and suboxide to the metallic state, the silver is reduced, and is precipitated in a dark-colored form by gallic or pyrogallic acid, in various degrees of strength, according to the extent of the reduction. The chief object and aim in the future of photography is in the direction of the developing agents. We have found substances which require but an instantaneous exposure to the action of light to effect that change, which, once set up, is continued and completed by suitable developing agencies.

SULPHURIC ACID.

Sulphuric acid may be formed by oxydizing sulphur with boiling nitric acid; but this plan would be too expensive to be adopted on a large scale. The commercial process for the manufacture of sulphuric acid is exceedingly ingenious and beautiful, but it involves reactions which are somewhat complicated, and do not admit of a superficial explanation.

Properties.—Anhydrous sulphuric acid is a white crystalline solid. The strongest liquid acid always contains one atom of water, which is closely associated with it, and cannot be driven off by the application of heat.

Sulphuric acid possesses intense chemical powers, and displaces the greater number of ordinary acids from their salts. It *chars* organic substances, by removing the elements of water, and converts alcohol into ether in a similar manner. The strength of a given sample of sulphuric acid may generally be calculated from its specific gravity, and a table is given by Dr. Ure for that purpose.

Impurities of Commercial Sulphuric Acid.—The liquid acid known as oil of vitriol is tolerably constant in composition, and seems to be as well adapted for photographic use as the pure sulphuric acid, which is far more expensive. The specific gravity should be about 1·836, at 60°. If a drop, evaporated upon platinum foil, gives a fixed residue, probably bisulphate of potash is present. A milkiness on dilution indicates sulphate of lead.

Test for Sulphuric Acid, either free or in combination with Bases.—If the presence of sulphuric acid, or soluble sulphate, is suspected in any liquid, it is tested for by adding a few drops of a dilute solution of chloride of barium or nitrate of baryta. A white precipitate, *insoluble in nitric acid*, indicates sulphuric acid. If the liquor to be tested is very acid, from nitric or hydrochloric acids, it must be largely diluted before testing, or a crystalline precipitate will form, caused by the sparing solubility of the chloride of barium itself in acid solutions.

ETHER.

Ether is obtained by distilling a mixture of sulphuric acid and alcohol. The term *sulphuric* applied to the commercial ether has reference only to the manner of its formation.

Properties of Ether.—It is neither acid nor alkaline to test-paper. Specific gravity at 60°, about ·720. Boils at 98° Fahrenheit. The vapor is exceedingly dense, and may be seen passing off from the liquid, and falling to the ground—hence the danger of pouring ether from one bottle to another, if a flame be near at hand.

Ether does not mix with water in all proportions—hence if the two are shaken together, after a short time the former rises and floats upon the surface. In this way a mixture of ether and alcohol may be separated from each other, as in the common process of *washing* ether. The water employed, however, always retains a certain portion of ether (about a tenth part of its bulk), and acquires a strong ethereal odor. Washed ether also contains water in small proportion.

Bromine and iodine are both soluble in ether, and gradually react upon and decompose it.

The strong alkalies, such as potash and soda,

also decompose ether slightly after a time, but not immediately. Exposed to air and light, ether is oxydized, and acquires a peculiar odor.

Ether dissolves fatty and resinous substances readily, but inorganic salts are mostly insoluble in this fluid; hence it is that iodide of potassium and other substances dissolved in alcohol are precipitated to a certain extent by the addition of ether.

WATER.

Water is an oxide of hydrogen, containing single atoms of each of the gases.

Distilled water is water which has been vaporized and again condensed; by this means it is freed from earthy and saline impurities, which are not volatile, and hence remain behind in the body of the retort. Pure water leaves no residue on evaporation, and should remain perfectly clear on the addition of nitrate of silver; also it should be neutral to test-paper.

Impurities of common Water.—Hard water, as it is termed, usually contains sulphate of lime and carbonate of lime, dissolved in carbonic acid; also chloride of sodium in greater or less quantity. On boiling the water, the carbonic acid gas is evolved, and the greater part of the carbonate of lime (if any is present) deposits, and forms an earthy incrustation on the boiler.

In testing water for sulphates and chlorides, acidify a portion with a few drops of *pure* nitric acid, free from chlorine; then divide it into two parts, and add to the first chloride of barium, and to the second nitrate of silver,—a milkiness, in either case, indicates the presence of impurity. The *photographic nitrate bath* cannot be used as a test for chlorides, since the iodide of silver it contains is precipitated on dilution.

Rain-water, having already undergone a natural process of distillation, is free from inorganic salts if collected in clean vessels; but it usually contains a minute portion of *ammonia*, and often organic matter, which tinges it of a brown color.

WEIGHTS AND MEASURES.

The weight generally employed in Photography is the apothecaries' weight; but some of the chemicals are sold by avoirdupois; for what reason no one can explain.

Nitrate of silver is usually sold by that weight, as well as most of the liquids. The acids and alkalies, however, are generally sold by apothecaries' weight.

APOTHECARIES' WEIGHT.

```
   1 grain.
  20 =   1 scruple
  60 =   3 =  1 drachm
 480 =  24 =  8 =  1 ounce
5760 = 288 = 96 = 12 = 1 pound.
```

AVOIRDUPOIS WEIGHT.

1 pound	= 16 ounces.
1 ounce	= 16 drachms.
1 drachm	= 26·343 grains.
(1 ounce avoirdupois	= 437·5 grains.)

IMPERIAL MEASURE.

1 gallon	= 8 pints.
1 pint	= 20 ounces.
1 ounce	= 8 drachms.

(1 fluid ounce of water weighs 437.5 grains, or 1 ounce avoirdupois.)

FLUID MEASURE.

1 minim				=	0·91	
60 =	1 fluid drachm			=	54·7 avoird.	
480 =	8 =	1 fluid ounce		=	437·5 =	1 oz.
9600 =	160 =	20 =	1 pint	=	8750 =	1.25 lb.
76,800 =	1280 =	160 =	8 = 2 gal'n =		70000 =	10 lbs.

(1 pound avoirdupois contains 7000 grains.)

1 pound Troy	.	.	.	contains	5760 grains.
1 imperial gallon of water	.	.	.	"	70,000 "
1 imperial pint of water contains 20 ounces, or					8750 "
1 cubic inch of water	"	"	"		252·4 "
1 ounce avoirdupois	.	"	"	"	437·5 "
1 ounce Troy	.	.	"	"	" 480 "
1 gramme	.	.	.	" " "	15·4 "
1 decigramme	.	.	"	" "	1·5 "
1 litre of distilled water	"	"	"		15,406·3 "

The grain is the unit of weight; but as three standards of weight are employed, much uncertainty and confusion often arise in the mind of the photographer as to which ounce or drachm is meant. The apothecaries' weight is generally understood to be the one employed; but it would save much trouble if the formulæ for the various preparations were always given in grains.

INDEX.

	PAGE
Albumen paper, to prepare	60
" " to silver	61
Ambrotypes on paper	170
" " on patent leather	155
Art, Photographic, History of the	19
Art, triumph of, over Nature	36
Ambrotype chemicals	38
" views, to take	170
Ambrotypes in the United States	34
" stereoscopic	152
" for lockets	169
" to color	166
" to darken	209
" to copy from Daguerreotypes	171
" apparatus for	131
Actino-Hydrometer for nitrate bath	136
Alcoholic solutions for collodions	182
Alcoholic solution of iodide of silver	183
" of bromide of silver	184
" of bromo-iodide of silver	185
" saturated, of iodide of potassium	186
" saturated, of bromide of potassium	187
Ammonia-nitrate of silver solution for positives	95
Acetic acid—its nature and properties	212
Alcohol—its nature and properties	213
Backgrounds, to print various shades	107
Bath, nitrate of silver, preparation of	133
" " to iodize	134

INDEX.

	PAGE
Bath, nitrate of silver, to test the	136
" " to neutralize	137
" " adding acid to	136
" gutta-percha, arrangement of	138
" flowing the	139
" renewal of the	140
" to keep the, in order	138
" silver, for chloride of sodium papers	59
" for toning and coloring	93, 94
" chloride of gold	93
" water, for positives	64
Backgrounds for Ambrotypes	176
Black and white specks on plates	197
Bromide of silver, alcoholic solution of	184
Bromo-iodide, alcoholic solution of	185
Bromide of potassium, saturated solution of	187
Bromine—its nature and properties	216
Bromide of potassium—its properties	216
Camera, time of exposure in the	46
" solar, for life size	70
" importance of a good	125
Collodion, negative, to prepare	82
" ammonia	82
" cadmium	82
" compound cadmium	83
" double iodized	84
" to remove water from	106
" to purify old	106
" to pour on the glass plate	146
" Ambrotype, preparation of	161
" to iodize, for Ambrotypes	162
" to be kept from the light	163
" tests of good	164
" to remove color from	164
" recipes for Ambrotypes	181
" to render any, highly sensitive	209
" for negatives, preparation of	82
" recipes for negatives	82-83
" mode of coating glass plates with	146
" first used	27
" signification of	27
" to preserve and keep ready for use	163
Chloroform for collodion	107
Copying Daguerreotypes into Photographs	69-70

INDEX.

	PAGE
Canada balsam, application of	155
Cautions in using chemicals, &c.	202
Cleaning the hands	204
" glass-plates for Ambrotypes	126
" " for negatives	41, 103
Chemicals, Ambrotype	132
" impurities of	200
Colors for Ambrotypes	167
Children's portraits, to take	177
Chloride of silver, adding to fixing solution	144
Cyanide of potassium, properties of	217
" " danger of using	203
Chloride of gold	213
Carbonate of soda	217
Daguerreotypes to copy life size	69–70
" " in Ambrotype	171
Diaphragm, use of	175
Developing solution for negatives	89
" " for iron Photographs	74
" " for Ambrotypes	141
" " various recipes for	143
" " for negatives	89
Dextrine paste for Photographs	104
Double glass process	152
Drying positive prints	67
" the picture	150
Enlarging pictures to life size	69
Engraving name on negatives	113
Engravings, to copy, in Ambrotype	173
Ether—its properties	230
" caution in using	203
Ether and alcohol to form collodion	160
Failure, causes of	194
Filtering process	135
Fixing solutions, preparations of, for Ambrotypes	144
Fixing bath for negatives	93, 44
" for positive paper	94
Fixing solution for negatives	44, 93
" for positives	94
Fogging the pictures	114, 195
" cause of, and to detect	114, 196

INDEX.

	PAGE
German process for negatives	85, 86, 87
Gum Arabic paste for positives	104
" " varnish for negatives	44
Glasses, preparation of, for Ambrotypes	126
" cleaning substances for	126
" cleaning new	127
" cleaning old	128
" cleaning, that have been varnished	129
" best adapted for Ambrotypes	130
" proper for negatives	47
" cleaning, for negatives	41
" to hold, after cleaning	45
Gun-cotton, discovery of	158
" preparation of	159
" test of acids employed for	160
" to wash and dry	160
" caution in preparing	203
Hints and suggestions on positives and negatives	112, 206
" " " " on paper	117
" " on negatives	112
History of Photography	19
Hydro-bromic acid, to prepare	187
Hydrometer, actino, for nitrate of silver bath	136
Hyposulphite of soda	219
" of gold	219
" of silver, to test its presence in positives	107
Iodine—its preparation and properties	220
Iodide of ammonia—its preparation and properties	224
" of potassium—its preparation and properties	222
" " alcoholic solution of	183
" of silver—its preparation and properties	223
" " alcoholic solution of	183
Iron Photographs, to make	73
Instantaneous printing	101
Imperfections in negatives	114
" in positives	120
Jewelry, to color, on Ambrotypes	168
Lampratype process	210
Light, to arrange, for Ambrotypes	174
" " for negatives	45

INDEX.

	PAGE
Light on the eyes, to arrange	176
Litmus—its nature and properties	225
Materials for Ambrotypes, in finishing	132
Machinery, to copy, in Ambrotype	173
Manipulations by the Ambrotype process	146, 147, 148, 149, 150
" by the negative process	41
Mounting Photographs	67
Melainotype plates	169
Negative process, theory of the	32
" practice of the	39
Negatives on glass	40
" definition of	40
" on glass, to take	41
" developing solutions for	43
" fixing solution for	44
" to develop	43
" frames to hold	45
" the color of	54
" silvery appearance of	116
Negative bath, the practice of the	51
" " changes of the	53
" collodions, to prepare	81, 82, 83
Nitrate of silver bath for negatives	48, 49
" " preparation of, for Ambrotypes	49
" " to iodize	49
" " to neutralize	137
Nitric acid—its nature and properties	225
Nitrate of potash—its nature and properties	226
Nitrate of silver—its nature and properties	226
Old collodion, to purify	106
" to remove water from	106
Pearl Ambrotypes, to make	210
Plates, to clean, on flat board	126
Plate-holders, varnish for	191
Plates, to hold, in proper position	147–148
Plate-holders necessary for Ambrotypes	125
Patent-leather process	155
Patent, Fox Talbot's, notice of	22
Plate-blocks for holding glasses	126
Plate-vise for holding glasses	126
Paper, Photographic, quality of	117

240 INDEX.

	PAGE
Paper, to dry salted	58
Practice of the negative process	39
Printing, instantaneous	101
" frames	109
Prints, to restore faded	102
" from negatives	62
" positives with chloride of sodium paper and pure silver	29
" " with ammonia-nitrate of silver	58
Photographic printing	56
" views	79-80
" process, theory of the	30
Photographs, to wash	65
" to mount	67
" to varnish	67
" to print	56
" positive, on glass	29
Photography—its history and progress	19
" its introduction into the United States	28
" chemicals first employed in	20
Pictures, negative and positive, on glass and paper	31
Positive process, theory of the	32
" fixing the	63
" washing the	65
" drying the	67
" mounting the	67
" printing the	62-63
Pyrogallic acid, solution for negatives	88
Protosulphate of iron—its nature and properties	224
Quick method of printing	93
Re-developing processes	87, 90, 92
Retouching negatives	113
" " for views	112
" positives on paper	119
Removing stains from the hands	204
" " from linen and clothes	205
Rehn's recipe for Ambrotype collodion	180
Statuary, to copy, in Ambrotype	173
Screens and backgrounds	175
" blue and white	177
Stains, to remove, from the hands	204
" to remove, from clothes	205
Single glass process	161

INDEX.

	PAGE
Silver, to add, to negative bath	52
Silver solution, plain	59
" " ammonia nitrate	95
Silver, to recover, from old solutions	103
Silvering the paper	58
Salting solutions for paper	57
Stereoscope pictures, to make	75, 76, 77, 78
" philosophy of the	76
Stereoscopic Ambrotypes	152
Skylight, arrangement of	174
Spots or streaks on plates	115, 200
Solutions, developing, for Ambrotypes	141, 142, 143
" " for negatives	87
Solution, alcoholic, of iodide of potassium	186
" " of bromide of potassium	187
" " of iodide of silver	183
" " of bromide of silver	184
" " of bromo-iodide of silver	185
Sulphuric acid—its nature and properties	228
" " impurities of	229
" " test of	229
Treble glass process	153
Transparent and opaque spots	198
Toning or fixing the print	63
" bath for positives on paper	93, 94
" " for iron Photographs	74
Transferring Ambrotypes on paper	170
Uncertainties of the art	55
Varnishing the pictures	152
Varnishes, to prepare	189
" applying the	192
Varnish, for negatives	44
" new, for Photographs	102
" to remove superfluous	156
" thick white, instead of Canada balsam	191
" used instead of Canada balsam	155
" white copal	189
" gum-demar	190
" black asphaltum	190
" white of shellac and copal	190
" gum-shellac, for plate-holders	191
Vocabulary of Photographic chemicals	211

	PAGE
Washing positive prints	65, 66, 118
" the positive pictures	65
Water, properties of	231
" impurities of	231
" distilled	231
Weights and Measures, tables of	233, 234
Window-glass for negatives	47

SCOVILL MANUFACTURING COMPANY,

4 BEEKMAN ST., N. Y.,

Manufacturers, Importers, and Dealers in all Articles pertaining to the Photographic, Ambrotype, and Daguerreotype Processes.

Scovill Manufacturing Co. have always on hand

A FULL ASSORTMENT OF

MATERIALS FOR PHOTOGRAPHS AND AMBROTYPES,

At WHOLESALE and RETAIL. Consisting of

CHEMICALS

Of the PUREST QUALITY, FULLY WARRANTED. Also,

APPARATUS, GUTTA PERCHA, PORCELAIN, and GLASSWARE,

of all kinds used in the Art;

CASES, MATTINGS, PRESERVERS, and GILT FRAMES,

Of every known pattern and finish. Together with all kinds of

Plate Glass,

Of White, ½ White, and other qualities, in large varieties.

Particular attention is called to the

CONVEX GLASS,

designed expressly for laying over Ambrotypes and Daguerreotypes, imparting to the Ambrotype a high artistic finish, even without the application of the white varnish. The utility of this Glass is pronounced unsurpassed by the most successful Artists, and it is sold as low as the ordinary Plate Glass.

Also, a New Article of highly polished

BLACK GLASS,

on which Ambrotypes are taken, superseding the necessity of using black varnish. This needs only to be known to be adopted.

Collodion (Iodized and Plain), **Gun Cotton, &c.,**

Made expressly for them by one of the most successful operators in the country.

Agents for Harrison's Improved Cameras, Tagliabue's Collodiometers, and Actino-Hydrometers for testing Chemicals, &c., &c.

Address......**SCOVILL MANUFACTURING CO.,**
4 BEEKMAN ST., NEW YORK.

HOLMES, BOOTH & HAYDENS,

MANUFACTURERS & IMPORTERS

OF EVERY VARIETY OF

AMBROTYPE,

DAGUERREOTYPE,

AND

PHOTOGRAPHIC GOODS,

OF THE

BEST QUALITY ONLY.

HOLMES, BOOTH AND HAYDENS'

CAMERAS,

From ¼ to mammoth size, warranted.

---

81 CHAMBERS STREET, NEW YORK.

Manufactory at Waterbury, Conn.

PURE CHEMICALS

FOR THE

AMBROTYPE, PHOTOGRAPHIC,

AND

DAGUERREIAN BUSINESS.

DEPOT FOR

Anthony's Celebrated Iodized Collodion for Ambrotypes,
Anthony's Iodized Collodion for Negatives,
" **Diamond Varnish** for Ambrotypes,
" **Negative Varnish,**
" **Photographic Varnish,**
" **Black Varnish,**
Pure Neutral Nitrate of Silver,
Pure Iodides of Potassium, Cadmium, & Ammonium,
" Bromides " " "
And Pure Chemicals of all kinds used in the Art.
Plate Glass for Ambrotypes, in great quantities, and of every quality.
Gutta Percha Baths, Trays, &c.
Ambrotype Preservers and Mattings.

An experience of seventeen years in the business gives us confidence in offering our goods. Catalogues furnished on application.

E. ANTHONY,

Manufacturer of Daguerreotype and Ambrotype Cases and Apparatus,

501 Broadway, New York.

AMBROTYPE SHIELDS ON HAND, AND MADE TO ORDER.

Agents for C. C. Harrison's Celebrated Cameras.

www.ingramcontent.com/pod-product-compliance
Lightning Source LLC
Chambersburg PA
CBHW020807230426
43666CB00007B/899